# *The Miracle Landing*

The true story of how the NBA's Minneapolis
Lakers almost perished in an Iowa cornfield
during a January blizzard

## Harold Gifford

Lieutenant Colonel, USAFR (Ret)

SIGNALMAN PUBLISHING

The Miracle Landing: The true story of how the NBA's
Minneapolis Lakers almost perished in an Iowa cornfield
during a January blizzard
by Harold Gifford

Signalman Publishing
www.signalmanpublishing.com
email: info@signalmanpublishing.com
Kissimmee, Florida

Cover design by Rob Cheney
Edited by Rachel Park
Interior layout and design by John McClure


ISBN: 978-1-935991-97-7 (Paperback)
978-1-935991-98-4  (ebook)

Library of Congress Control Number: 2013936024

SIGNALMAN
PUBLISHING

# DEDICATION

To my wife, Carol, who has kept me on the ball with her encouraging support and helpful suggestions, and to my brother, Quentin, who—before dying at Pearl Harbor—had me headed in the right direction by his motivating act of brotherly love. Had I not heeded his advice, my life would have been completely different. Also to our passengers who bravely kept it all together and suffered the cold, severe discomfort, and fear during their longest night.

# ACKNOWLEDGMENTS

I owe a great debt of gratitude to the U.S. Army Air Corps and the U.S. Air Force Reserve that I was privileged serve for 29 years. Without their world's best training, I may not have survived.

John Steffes of Carroll lighted the spark that turned into a flame that still burns in my life.

Doug Burns, editor and owner of the *Carroll Daily Times Herald*, deserves credit for inciting the flurry of media coverage of an event that occurred over fifty years ago.

Last but not least, my thanks to the wide awake young pilot who helped save all of our lives. If Jim Holznagel hadn't been in the cockpit that night, we very likely would all have perished.

Jim Holznagel (on the left) and myself at our reunion in 2010.

# FOREWORD

I first met Harold Gifford in person in Carroll, Iowa when I was honored with an invitation to the Lakers Basketball Court dedication to commemorate the 50th anniversary of "the miracle landing". The true story Harold tells in this book is almost too hard to believe—that a larger than life team such as the Lakers would ever go through an ordeal like that. It defied the odds that everyone not only survived but literally got up and walked away. Each time I hear the story, it's still scary even fifty years later. Had the team been wiped out that night instead of safely landing, it's my personal belief that the franchise would not have recovered and would have folded. No doubt there would eventually have been an NBA team in Los Angeles but it would not have been the LAKERS. Had future Hall of Famer Elgin Baylor and the other team members perished, it would have completely altered the future of the Lakers.

When people ask me, "Where did the name 'Lakers' come from?" I tell them the team originated in Minneapolis – the land of 10,000 lakes. Now I add to the story of the miracle landing and of a hero, and a personal friend, named Harold Gifford. It's a turning point of Lakers history and the more the fans know about their team the more they love us.

It was exciting that we could dedicate a basketball court in the place that will forever play a role in the Lakers storyline and it also adds to my personal goal of making the Lakers America's team. We now have a sister city in Carroll, Iowa, where kids are playing the game of basketball on a Lakers court. This book tells a fascinating piece of history, of heroic efforts that not only saved a basketball team, but saved the lives of 23 men, women and children. Because of this miracle landing, these folks would be able to continue their lives with their families and loved ones for the next half century. Enjoy the read, but, most of all, be inspired!

Jeanie Buss
Executive Vice President
Los Angeles Lakers

# ABOUT THE AUTHOR AND CO-PILOT

# "AN AVIATOR'S AVIATOR"

Millions are spent each year training professional pilots to perform with the skill and precision of a brain surgeon. While performing their duties, they are responsible for making critical decisions on a regular basis. To this end these dedicated professionals conform to a lifestyle that ensures optimum performance at all times when on duty.

### A Word by Patrick Moran

I met Harold Gifford in 2010 while I was serving as president of the Minnesota Business Aviation Association (MBAA). While searching for a speaker for one of our monthly lunch meetings, I received several recommendations from members to ask Harold if he would speak about his aviation career. At around the same time, Harold was gaining notoriety due to the recent 50-year anniversary of the amazing January 18, 1960 successful Iowa cornfield landing of a crippled DC-3 with members of the Minneapolis Lakers team aboard. Harold agreed to speak, and he and I met several times before the lunch to prepare notes for his talk. I became fascinated with the DC-3 story, but to say that's all that was fascinating about Harold would be inaccurate.

I learned about his early flying career, including WWII Army Air Corps service as a fighter pilot gunnery instructor and flying as third pilot and Flight Engineer on B-29s over the Pacific; post-military crop dusting in Montana and Idaho; flying charter and corporate airplanes and helicopters; and finally his Air Force Reserve service flying P-51 Mustangs, F-80 jet fighters, C-119 Flying Boxcars and C-130s for the Air Force Reserve. The list of airplanes he has flown throughout his career is long and diverse, spanning a wide range of missions. And just as amazing as his hugely varied flying career has been his personal life story, from owning and operating a Texaco gas station to blowing glass for neon signs; from selling real estate and securities in Florida and real estate in Minnesota to establishing submarine sandwich shops in Florida and establishing and operating a business brokerage firm in Florida.

As for Harold's MBAA lunch talk, he was a huge hit! I received many appreciative comments from members who thoroughly enjoyed his stories. The word got out, and Harold went on to speak at several other aviation meetings for different organizations in the near future for which I assisted with a slide show presentation. His talks were always as well received as at our MBAA luncheon.

Harold has been a huge inspiration to me personally and professionally. His passionate yet humorous storytelling of flying in the "glory days" of aviation is almost unbelievable to those of us who fly today's high-tech airplanes. I think what has impressed me most about Harold is his perseverance through adversity and as a caregiver and obvious pride in his accomplishments, both in aviation and in his personal life. I am forever indebted to Harold for sharing his stories with me and many aviation organizations in the past few years. Thanks, Harold!"

—Patrick Moran, retired USCG officer and pilot, corporate pilot; Gulfstream, Plymouth, Minnesota.

### Military Aircraft Flown
Interstate Cadet
PT-19 primary trainer
BT-13 basic trainer, navigation and instrument
AT-6 Texan advanced, formation and gunnery
P-40 Warhawk
B-29 Superfortress
L-2 Liason
L-4 Liason
P-51 Mustang fighter
P-80 jet fighter
T-33 jet trainer
C-119 Flying Boxcar
C-130 Hercules

### Private and Civilian Aircraft Flown
Aeronca pre-WW II-54 B
Aeronca Champion
Piper Cub
Piper Tri-Pacer (owned)
Piper Apache
Piper Comanche
Beech Musketeer
Beech Bonanza
Beech Debonair
Beech Travelair

Beech Twin Bonanza

Beech C-45

Beech D-18

Beech E-18 S

Beech Queen Air

Beech King Air 90

Beech King Air A-90

Beech King Air 200

Beech Jet (Mitsubishi)

Cessna 150

Cessna 170

Cessna 172

Cessna 180

Cessna 182

Cessna 195

Cessna 210

Cessna 310

Cessna 421

Luscombe Silvaire (owned)

Mooney M-20 and 21

Navion

Lockheed Lodestar

Commander 400

Commander Turboprop

Commander Jet 1121

Learjet 120

Saberliner Jet-60

Hughes 269-A helicopter

Hughes 300 helicopter

**Pilot Ratings**

Single engine, multi engine, instrument, rotorcraft, air transport pilot, Air Force command pilot, type rated in 1121 Commander jet.

At one time I was current in and frequently flying several various types of airplanes, including heavy twin tricycle gear, heavy twin tail-dragger, medium twin tail-dragger, light twin, single-engine tail dragger, single-engine tricycle gear, jet-powered, turboprop and helicopter. I had memorized a checklist that I always used as a final review before taking the runway even though the regular checklist for the airplane had been read—SCIGFTPR: **S** for seatbelts, windows, doors, and hatches; **C** for controls free; **I** for check instruments; **G** for gas or fuel management; **F** for proper wing or cowl flap setting; **T** for trim tabs set; **P** for propeller control position; **R** for run up engines .

### A Word by Tom Roe

I was fortunate to fly with Giff in the Air Force Reserve in Minneapolis for many years where we flew the C-119 and the C-130. The C-119 was a reciprocating two engine, non-pressurized aircraft that was used by the Air Force to haul cargo or troops, usually for air drops. It was a fairly reliable aircraft when supported by superior maintenance, as our aircraft fortunately was in the 934th Tactical Airlift Group. After the C-119 was phased out around the early 1970s we were given the C-130A model aircraft to fly. This was a four engine, turbine-powered aircraft with much higher operating airspeed and altitude limitations when compared to the C-119.

When we received the C-130, Giff flew the first one into

Minneapolis from Houston and was later selected by the 934th Commander as project officer to help develop and implement a combat training program for flight operations. Giff then became the first combat training instructor, selecting the most qualified to lead in training their departments.

Aided by his efforts in flight operations, the 934th Tactical Airlift Group was the first Reserve or National Guard C-130 Unit to achieve combat-ready status. The 934th was selected as the Outstanding Air Force Reserve Unit in the nation for 1971, and Giff was awarded the Air Force Commendation Medal for his work as project officer. Giff was later assigned as interim Commander of the 934th Group.

I flew many trips with Giff both in the states and out of the country, usually trips to Fort Benning, Georgia for training air drops in support of the Army jump school or cargo flights to Air Force bases around the country or to Puerto Rico, Panama, Alaska, Newfoundland and Bermuda.

With the C-119, we were usually flying at flight levels below 10,000 feet due to our lack of pressurization. This put us into the weather quite often. The C-130 operated at higher altitudes and usually provided a much smoother flight. When it came to flying weather, Giff was the pilot you wanted on your flight. He had a knack for being able to pick his way through the cold fronts containing virtually solid thunderstorms across our route of flight. He had a number of theories to accomplish transit of these troublesome areas on our route, and of all the times his theories were tested I don't recall he ever failed to avoid the storms. We had radar on the C-130 but the C-119 had nothing other than Giff's quiet study of the visual appearance of the storm followed by a decision to turn left, right or go straight ahead. To me the options all looked the same but his choice usually produced the desired results.

We also picked up a fair amount of ice on the C-119 being at the low altitudes where ice was more commonly encountered. Fortunately the C-119 had heated leading edge wings, heated booms and prop de-ice. However, we still frequently encountered ice buildups had to be careful to avoid heavy icing. Again, Giff had the ability to pick the right altitude to avoid the worst icing levels. Sometimes it called for a climb and other times a descent.

Flying with Giff was always an enjoyable experience. He was a very knowledgeable, professional pilot who knew his business and enjoyed flying. He knew the aircraft and was well aware of its limitations. He was always ready with a good story involving a charter flight or the reserve. One usually filled with humor, Giff had an ability to tell a story over the intercom that kept the entire crew entertained. Our flights with Giff were always interesting, enjoyable experiences, not only for me but also for the rest of the crew.

We carried two pilots, one navigator, one flight engineer and a loadmaster. Our flight engineer Bob Otto had arranged to hook up a popcorn popper and electric roaster for first class meals such as prime rib sandwiches, baked chicken or ham on those long flights. We all had our jobs to perform but those were very entertaining flights and I remember all of them.

—Tom Roe, Col. USAF (Ret.)

## A Word by Don Rott

My friendship with Harold Gifford began in 1960 when we were both employed by Gopher Aviation, a Beechcraft distributor and Hughes helicopter dealer. Giff was in the charter department and I was in sales. As charter manager, Giff organized Canadian fly-in fishing and hunting trips. They were very popular and often featured on WCCO's TV show "World of Aviation," which was hosted by the late Sherm Booen.

In addition to his charter management duties, Giff provided pilot and flight services for corporations. After selling larger airplanes to corporations, Gopher would provide pilot service when needed.

Some memorable highlights flying with Giff include the following:

Test-hopping many different types of aircraft for the maintenance department, including a Lockheed Hudson Bomber, now called a Lodestar that Giff checked himself out in with the aid of a mechanic who had worked on the bomber in WW II. He then flew for my sales demonstration when I was trying to sell the airplane.

A trip to Washington D.C. flying a Twin Beech in turbulent weather while he picked his way around thunderstorms with nervous passenger Bob Short, owner of the Lakers. The trip included some perks, including an invitation to Senator Hubert Humphrey's office and touring the Air and Space Museum.

Jumping in a couple of helicopters when Giff called and getting our daily 'buzz job' out of the way. We often landed on the edge of the swimming pool at the Golden Steer restaurant in

South St. Paul for lunch. We were always welcome to land in the parking lot at McGuire's supper club for lunch—we would draw a crowd.

Landing with two helicopters in Gordy Campbell's yard overlooking the Minnesota River Valley in the fall, blowing leaves everywhere. There were many other interesting stories.

Harold is a Aviator's Aviator, a Pilot's Pilot. He is a great storyteller and his book should be an interesting read for anyone.

It is my good fortune to be Giff's friend and we still get together for lunch and 'open up the hangar door' to reminisce over the many fun flying experiences we had shared.

We both enjoy swapping books about aviation and Giff recently shared a book, ***The Blonde Knight of Germany***, which is the story of Eric Hartman, a German Fighter pilot who had shot down more airplanes than anyone in the history of aerial warfare—352 confirmed kills. Giff had the pleasure of treating Eric Hartman to dinner in 1971. Spending ten years in a Russian prison after the war, Hartman was selected to help operate the West German Air Force. Hartman toured Air Force units in the U.S. to learn what he could, and while Giff was serving as Commander of the 934th he visited that unit. Giff enjoys telling about what a very interesting person Hartman was.

Giff has remained active in flying, having invested in a fleet of helicopters, but he drives his wife Carol and yorkie Chloe nuts as they fly around the house crashing into furniture and falling to the floor. He tells me that he flies the F-15 now and then on his X-Box and he nearly becomes airborne flying his two huge kites with his grandchildren.

—Don Rott, aircraft sales

# CONTENTS

# INTRODUCTION
# "THE REAL, TRUE STORY"

Imagine—what if you were the co-pilot on a DC-3 with twenty-three souls on board when shortly after take-off, into a dark and stormy Missouri sky, the cockpit lights went dim, then bright, flickered, then out. You were still in the clouds and it became completely dark in the cockpit and cabin. The flashlight that you had on your lap revealed that the aircraft had a total failure of the electrical system. Of much greater concern was seeing that the captain, after reaching up to turn off the battery switch, had released the control column and did not appear to be responding to the emergency. Perhaps he had done this knowing that he had trimmed the airplane to continue climbing on its own, hands off. He was very quiet and had little to say about the situation. Think about it—what would you have done?

The following is a story about one particular incident that occurred during my fifty-year flying career. It was the most harrowing and memorable experience that I can recall from many years as a pilot.

The story is mostly about a famous professional basketball team, the Minneapolis Lakers; a famous airplane, the Douglas DC-3; a famous town in Iowa, Carroll; and a flight crew: Verne Ullman, Jim Holznagel and myself.

When I tell you that this flight occurred over fifty years ago, you might ask, "Why is it of so much interest after all those years, other than the fact many younger aviation and Lakers enthusiasts have not heard about it?" My reply is the following account.

In 2009 a sports editor, Peter Vecsey of the *New York Post*, went to Los Angeles to interview Elgin Baylor about his illustrious career in basketball and his having been inducted into the NBA Hall of Fame. During the course of the interview, Elgin mentioned that he had been a passenger on the DC-3 that Bob Short had purchased in order to transport the team in a more practical and affordable manner. Elgin had referred to a certain harrowing experience on one of those flights. Peter then had become interested in hearing Elgin's account of the event. Here is a good story, he thought, and decided on a plan to interview other players who had been on the flight and to write a story about the event. That story was published in the *New York Post* in February 2009.

John Steffes of Carroll, Iowa, an avid sports historian, received a copy of this story from a friend living in New York. After reading the story, John realized that January 18, 2010 would be the fiftieth anniversary of the incident and he then began to consider some sort of commemorative event.

I and Jim Holznagel were invited to attend the event in Carroll, Iowa on January 18, 2010. (The pilot, Verne Ullman, had died from a brain tumor in March 1965.) The commemorative event would feature Jim and I telling our story of the flight and the unveiling of a large plaque commemorating the incident. Several of the local people who witnessed the event would be there to tell their story. This event, having been promoted by John Steffes, resulted in a flurry of media attention both locally and nationally.

Recently, Jim was asked by a reporter if he would be available for an interview. Jim's response was, "Do you want to hear the real, true story about the event or the often-published version?" Jim's offer had been declined. After the event, Jim and I—for various reasons—had decided to move on and not make any waves. Since then, Jim and I decided that it was time to set the record straight. This book is the complete account of what happened to the flight carrying the Minneapolis Lakers that left St. Louis bound for Minnesota on January 17, 1960.

# 1

# A CAREER IN AVIATION

Charles Lindbergh was once asked why he chose flying as a career and his answer was in four parts:

1. Science and technology—that is what every aspect of flying is about.
2. Adventure—unimagined and unpredicted experiences and adventures will present themselves.
3. Beauty—landscape artists would love to be able to view the many awesome beauties of this planet from low levels and extremely high altitudes.
4. Freedom—as in the poem *High Flight* written by Gillespie Magee:

> "Oh! I have slipped the surly bonds of Earth,
> And danced the skies on laughter-silvered wings;
> Sunward I've climbed, and joined the tumbling mirth
> Of sun-split clouds—and done a hundred things
> You have not dreamed of—wheeled and soared and swung
> High in the sunlit silence. Hovering there,
> I've chased the shouting wind along, and flung
> My eager craft through footless halls of air,
> Up, up the long, delirious, burning blue
> I've topped the wind-swept heights with easy grace,

Where never lark, or even eagle flew;
And, while with silent, lifting mind I've trod
The high untrespassed sanctity of space,
Put out my hand, and touched the face of God."

My dog, Ring, and I were sitting on a fallen log as we watched squirrels gathering nuts for winter. The quiet of the warm autumn morning was interrupted by a strange, roaring sound. The sound grew steadily louder and then for the first time in my life, when I was nearly six, I saw an airplane. As the red bi-plane flew by the pilot spotted me and waved his hand. I ran to the old barn and climbed to the top as I watched the airplane become a speck in the clear blue sky. My imagination and curiosity were kindled as I wondered who the pilot was. It was 1929, two years after Charles Lindbergh's historical flight—could it be Charles Lindbergh?

I was thrilled and excited as I ran to the house to tell my mother about what I had seen. She had not heard it as she had the old gasoline engine-powered Maytag washer popping away. From that moment, my heart filled with longing to fly.

In 1931, we moved from the farm to Comfrey, Minnesota, a very small town, and we now had a small Crosley radio. It was exciting to hurry home from school to listen to "The Air Adventures of Jimmie Allen," which always began with the explosive then fading roar of an airplane engine as in a dive.

At a Fourth of July celebration in Comfrey, a barnstorming pilot had flown over and after a few loops he glided to a landing not far from town. Immediately hitting the road, I found where the plane had landed. I was awed by the activity of passengers laughing and giggling with joy after a ride in the open cockpit. The odor from engine exhaust, the roar of the engine, and the blast of the propeller kicking up dust and grass was exhilarating. While landing with the throttle retarded, a different sound could be heard. The now soft purr of the engine and whistling of air over the wings and struts was like music to my ears. No doubt about it, this was for me.

In the display window of a nearby Skelly gas station was a bright red rubber band-powered model airplane, which was offered on a promotion to gas customers. I wanted one but unfortunately our family did not have a car.

In 1935 my family moved to Mankato, Minnesota, which was exciting for an eleven-year-old to move to a larger town—this town had an airport and stores to buy airplane models. One of the first I bought was "The Spirit of Saint Louis."

I'll never forget the greatest of all my models, a thirty-six inch wingspan rubber band-powered monoplane with a propeller that folded when the rubber power was exhausted and became a sailplane. The nearby airport had a lot of open space for model flying. Using a hand power drill with a hook on the end to wind up the rubber, I launched this bright yellow masterpiece. It was a hot summer day and it kept climbing and circling until it became a sailplane, and caught up in a thermal, it headed south while ascending. I jumped on a bicycle and tried to follow my bird, but it was a goner. After an extensive search over the next few days I had to accept the inevitable.

On my fourteenth birthday, my dad surprised me with a trip to the nearby airport and my first airplane ride. We climbed into the Stinson and secured our seat belts as the pilot cranked up the engine and began taxiing to the runway. We became airborne and climbed higher, as the buildings and cars below grew smaller. I was surprised by the lack of a sense of speed—it seemed we went slower as we climbed. Our airspeed was nearly ninety miles an hour. We circled the city identifying familiar places including our home with five acres of garden where I spent a lot of time weeding and hoeing. I fully realized that this is what I wanted to do.

The following summer, in 1935, I saw a tri-motor airplane circling to land at the nearby airport. I jumped on a bike and hurried to the airport where I saw the huge bird with the corrugated metal fuselage in all its glory, its three engines still creaking as they cooled. The pilots with their high boots, riding britches and leather jackets were an awesome sight. I talked to the pilots and learned that they were seasoned veterans of the skies who just a few years prior had survived flying the mail in old crates in extremely difficult and dangerous conditions. Many of these guys had died with their boots on. These wise old birds had saved what they could and invested in the Ford tri-motor. Barnstorming was a safer and more profitable way to make a living.

I asked if there was anything that I could do to earn a ride and they showed me a sign advertising airplane rides. I was told that if I would carry the sign up and down the main street I could go up with them. After over an hour of sweating, I thought it time for a payoff.

When I saw the big bird headed for a landing, I hurried to the airport and was told to climb in. I sat between the two engines on the wings, just behind the cockpit. There was a small window to look out and enjoy the sights. I watched the seasoned pilots at work and with great admiration. I envied them. After a bumpy landing in a strong crosswind, we were out of the airplane and I headed back to town with my sign. By the end of the day, I had earned two more rides in the noisy old bird and was thrilled but exhausted from carrying the sign and hiking to the airport and back. The best payoff was when the head pilot gave me a pat on the back and said I had done a great job. With four rides under my belt at this time I felt as though I was on my way to a career in aviation.

During the next seven years prior to WW II, I had built many model airplanes that flew, read all the aviation books I could find, and saw all the flying movies. My desire was being nourished to a fever pitch and in the spring of 1940 I left high school to work on a dairy farm to earn money for flying lessons. I was paid $35.00 a month with room and board and every other Sunday off. I had never worked so hard in my life but I had a goal in mind.

Flying is a serious business. Enthusiasm and ability to perform and achieve are based on knowledge and one can never have too much of it.

In 1940, my older brother, Quentin, had been home on leave from the Navy. I had been able to spend some quality time with him on my days off. On the day that he had to return to his ship,the Battleship USS OKLAHOMA (BB-37), at Bremerton, Washington, my Dad brought him to the dairy farm where I worked to say goodbye. Quentin said to me, "After discussing your situation the other day, I have a plan."

"What's on your mind ?" I asked.

"Here's the deal, If you will promise to go back to Loyola, work hard and graduate from high school, I will make a promise to you that when I'm out of the Navy, I'll find a way for us to get a college degree and if you don't do this I will be disappointed in you." We weren't much into hugging in those days but Quentin embraced me and told me he loved me and cared about me. Choked up with emotion, I gave him my solemn promise. We said goodbye for the last time. Quentin went back to his ship and I eventually went back to Loyola High School in Mankato, worked very hard and made very good grades.

Right: My mother, brother
(Quentin), and I in 1940.

# 2

# THE U.S. ARMY
# AIR CORPS

The war and the Army Air Corps launched a career in aviation that would span fifty years.

In December 1942, a year after the bombing of Pearl Harbor, I applied for enlistment in the U.S. Army Air Corps. Expecting a long war, the various branches of service were competing for enlistment of potential candidates for flight training though they did not have space in the training pipeline to handle them at the time. To overcome this problem, they contracted with colleges throughout the U.S. to accommodate the new recruits. An active duty military cadre was assigned to these schools to establish military and college training for the recruits.

My hard work in school paid off; I scored very high in the rigorous and comprehensive testing and during the last week of December 1942, I was sworn in as an Aviation Student of the U.S. Army Air Corps. On February 3, 1943, after a tearful goodbye to Mom and my sisters, Dad drove me to the train depot in Mankato. I was the last of three sons to be consumed by the war effort and I can understand how they felt. Life for all would never again be the same.

The train took me to St. Paul, where I boarded a troop train headed for Jefferson Barracks, Missouri to acquire Basic Army training. The first night at J. B. we were all still in our civilian clothing and the barracks we were housed in were very basic and cold. I used my winter overcoat as an extra blanket. The next morning, we were lined up in a marching formation and marched to a mess hall where we had our first introduction to army fare. After a hearty breakfast of flapjacks, eggs and sausage, we were marched to a big auditorium where we were told what we would be doing here. We were then issued uniforms and clothing and lined up for inoculations, and then the VD films, lectures and reading of the articles of war. We were soon on the drill field learning our left foot from our right. This became a daily activity until we became proficient at it. Wherever we went, it was in formation with a leader calling cadence.

After two weeks of basic, we were allowed to go into St. Louis for a night out. For the very first time in my life I bought a steak at a restaurant. I could choose my steak from a meat counter and have it cooked the way I wanted it. I had a sirloin, baked potato and salad and the bill came to $1.50.

Another week of marching and I learned I'd be going to Kansas State University in Manhattan, Kansas. About twenty-four of us were bunked in a fraternity house near campus. We soon began a full schedule of academic studies, consisting mostly of science, math and meteorology. In addition, we had athletic and military training.

After our two-week quarantine we were allowed a weekend off. The sororities had made plans for welcoming parties and social activities for us on our first free time but many guys just wanted go to town and have a few beers. For those who showed up at the sorority party, there were more than enough pretty girls to go around for dancing and partying. Some of the guys who went to town wished they had stayed for the parties as the guys who stayed met some classy chicks and had a grand time.

After three months of college life, it was back on a troop train for San Antonio, Texas. Three days later I awoke to the sweet scent of blue bonnets in bloom after a morning shower. This sure beat the bitter cold of the Midwest. We were on a railroad siding near San Antonio awaiting transportation to the Cadet Classification Center near Kelly Field.

We were quartered in regular military barracks, with forty-eight men to a building. Wherever we went, we marched in twelve columns of four. The food in the mess hall was better than at J.B. but not quite as good as the cafeteria at Kansas State. It was here that we underwent days of testing to determine what we were best qualified to do in the Army Air Corps. We were subjected to every kind of testing imaginable from problem solving to hand eye coordination and general I.Q. testing. The weirdest of all was the psychiatrist interview. He really got into personal stuff about my sex life and sexual experiences—did I have girlfriends and if so did I have sex, did I hate my father or mother, did I masturbate. This was scary stuff for a kid from a Catholic school where the only time I talked about this stuff was in the confessional. These guys didn't give me any penance for my perceived indiscretions.

Most guys hoped to qualify for fighter pilot training as that had the most glamour and promised to be the most fun and exciting. For the next few days, everyone anxiously checked the bulletin board for the results. Many did not make it for flight training for various reasons—color blindness, poor coordination, and other reasons. These unfortunates were assigned to gunnery school, aircraft mechanic school and other ground duties. Some were selected for navigator or bombardier school, and others for multi-engine or single engine training. I was ecstatic when my name appeared on the fighter pilot training list.

I would now be an Aviation Cadet with the title of "Mister". The next phase of training would be pre-flight school.

Imagine the thrill of a nineteen-year-old aviation cadet wearing a brown leather flying suit and white silk scarf, helmet with goggles hanging and parachute slung over his shoulder as he walked with his instructor on the flight line. Imagine the sight of a long row of beautiful blue and yellow open cockpit training airplanes as we approach the one where I will have my first flight with the U.S. Army Air Corps.

After 10 hours of flight instruction, I made my first solo flight on Nov 19,1943, a date that I'll never forget. A total of 65 hours flying time was spent learning basic flight maneuvers and aerobatics then it was on to Garden City, Kansas.

The next nine weeks were spent in Basic Flight training at Garden City flying the Vultee BT-13 for another seventy hours of flight training. We learned instrument, formation and night flying. The nine weeks after that were spent in Advanced Flight training at Eagle Pass, Texas flying the North American AT-6 Texan for another eighty hours and then on to graduation as a pilot and a commission as an officer with the rank of Second Lieutenant.

The next phase was transition to the P-40 fighter and aerial gunnery in the AT-6. After completing that, I became a fighter pilot gunnery instructor. However, the war in Europe soon began winding down so fighter pilot training was curtailed and I began a new course of training to become a flight engineer and third pilot on a B-29 bomber. After serving in the South Pacific on a B-29, I returned to the U.S. and was discharged from active duty but continued to serve as a pilot in the Air Force Reserve.

I became a licensed commercial pilot and spent a summer as an air taxi pilot flying in an Aeronca Champion, and also crop dusting with a Piper Cub in Montana and Idaho. While in the Air Force Reserve, I resumed flying fighter aircraft—specifically the P-51 Mustang and P-80 Shooting Star. However, the Pentagon decided to change our mission so our fighters were eventually replaced by the twin engine C-119—also known as the Flying Boxcar. After putting many more hours of flight time, I was able to upgrade my civilian pilot certificate to multi-engine and instrument ratings leading to my becoming employed by Gopher Aviation as an air taxi pilot.

During WW II, the Air Corps fighter command published a monthly report titled "Hairy Tales." On its cover was a god-awful looking creature with a long hairy tail, wearing a helmet and goggles. This publication contained reports of close calls and scary experiences as reported by pilots in combat.

Pilots in general often refer to a frightening experience as a *hairy tale*. I have begun writing a book about the many such experiences throughout my flying career as well as other details about my life.

# 3

# NEW ASSIGNMENT: LAKERS' CO-PILOT

Not long after WW II, there were several attempts to establish professional basketball leagues and franchises in the U.S. Not until 1949 was real success attained when the BBA (Basketball Association of America) merged with the NBL (National Basketball League) forming the NBA (National Basketball Association). Initially there were seventeen teams in the league including the Detroit Gems. Two Minneapolis businessmen bought the Detroit franchise for $15,000, which had a miserable four and forty 1948 season. After moving the franchise to Minneapolis, the name of the team was changed to the Minneapolis Lakers. While still in the BBL, the Lakers won the 1948 championship and then went on to win NBA Championships in 1949, 1950, 1952, 1953 and 1954. Eventually only eight teams survived in the NBA: the Minneapolis Lakers, the Boston Celtics, the Detroit Pistons, the St. Louis Hawks, the Cincinnati Royals, the Philadelphia Warriors, the Syracuse Nationals, and the N.Y. Knickerbockers. Today there are thirty teams in the NBA.

In the following section is a fascinating history of the Lakers that I thought would be helpful to include in this book to give the reader the proper context of the time—1960. Also included in sections throughout the book are bios of some of the players.

## A Brief History of the Lakers
( used with permission from Lakers.com)

The patriarch and founding father of the Laker franchise is the ubiquitous Sid Hartman. In 1946, at the age of 26, Hartman was employed by a Minneapolis newspaper. It was Hartman's practice to buy newspapers from other cities to keep up with the world of sports. Hartman learned the Detroit Gems franchise was about fold. In order to test the market for professional basketball, Hartman—along with businessmen Mike Alpert and Ben Berger—had a plan. They brought in the professional teams from Oshkosh and Sheboygan, Wisconsin for an exhibition game. The game, played at the Minneapolis Auditorium, was a success and drew five thousand fans.

Hartman then approached Minneapolis businessmen Morris Chalfen and Ben Berger about buying the Detroit team and moving it to Minneapolis. When they agreed Hartman flew to Detroit, met the owner at the airport, giving him the $15,000 check after signing the agreement. The new "Minneapolis Lakers," named for the land of ten thousand lakes, were set to join the NBL for the 1947-1948 season. Berger wanted Hartman to quit the paper and run the Lakers as the general manager but Hartman chose otherwise. In those days reporters were not paid very much and the editors had no problem with reporters having another job on the side. Chalfen and Berger decided that since Hartman didn't care to work full time they needed a business manager.

A month before the beginning of the season, they brought in Max Winter, promoter and owner of the 620 Club on Hennepin

Avenue, famous as the place "Where Turkey is King." Winter took care of the business end and Hartman was in charge of basketball. This worked out well and they became lifetime friends. Hartman was in charge of getting the players and he got off to a good start by signing Jim Pollard, a great forward from Stanford. Hartman convinced the owners to come up with $15,000 to buy the rights to Tony Jaros and Don Carlson.

Chicago had a team called the Gears who signed the famous big man George Mikan from DePaul University. The Gears later folded, and because the Detroit Gems had finished last in the BBL there was no doubt about the Lakers rights to Mikan. Hartman and company convinced Mikan to fly to Minneapolis. He wanted $12,000 to sign—a lot of money in 1947. The meeting ended and Mikan was scheduled on the last flight to Chicago. Hartman and Winter talked it over and figured if he made that flight he was gone for good. Hartman drove Mikan to the airport and strangely he got lost or encountered a traffic delay and Mikan missed his flight. They put him up in a downtown hotel then brought him to the Lakers office the next morning and agreed to pay him the $12,000. Mikan joined the Lakers for the second game of the season beginning a dynasty that lasted until 1954. Hartman also hired the St. Thomas College coach, John Kundla, for twice the salary he was getting from St. Thomas.

During the late fifties Minnesota fans tired of the Lakers' losing ways and attendance dropped badly. The Lakers had been playing in two different ancient arenas in Minneapolis and St. Paul, which had added to the lack of interest in attending games.

## Elgin Baylor

The history of Elgin's achievements would require several pages, including his induction into the Hall of Fame and his many years in coaching and management after retiring from playing.

Bob Short admitted that without Elgin, his Laker franchise would have faced bankruptcy. That proves that the cornfield episode was not the only savior of the franchise.

On the long flights to the east coast, when all others were asleep, Elgin often came up to the cockpit and visited with us. He would ask about where we were at the moment, what was the weather like en route and how high we were. He seemed to enjoy looking down upon the landscape from nearly two miles up as we pointed out the cities that we were flying over. Elgin's keen interest in these things led me to think that he secretly would like to fly as a pilot.

As I often watched Elgin in games on the road, I noticed an unusual habit. After racing down the sidelines as he was about to make his famous hook shot, he'd turn his head slightly away from the basket. Other players claimed it was a habit he acquired from playing cards as he grabbed a peek into the hand held by the player sitting next to him. That was not really true; Elgin was one of the nicest guys and was very well liked by all the players.

I had always looked forward to his visits to the front office. I can recall his unique laugh as they played cards when something had obviously gone his way. Those were some very fun times for me.

Team photo of the 1958-59 Lakers. Seated left to right: Boo Ellis, Jim Krebs, Bob Burrow, Vern Mikkelsen, Elgin Baylor, Steve Hamilton. Standing left to right: John Kundla (coach), Dick Garmaker, "Hot Rod" Hundley, Ed Fleming, Slick Leonard.

Of this group, Ellis, Krebs, Baylor, Garmaker, Hundley, and Leonard were on the flight of January 17-18, 1960. (courtesy LA Lakers)

Photo (right) of Elgin Baylor being congratulated by Lakers owner Bob Short and his teammates upon joining the Lakers in 1958. (courtesy Brian Short)

Bob Short came into the picture when he and partners paid $150,000 for the team. In an attempt to overcome this problem, Short had dreamed up various promotions. One of them was to give as a door prize a Shetland pony in hopes that kids would drag their parents to games. That didn't help and Brian Short recently told me that they had a lot of ponies grazing in their yard in Edina. Ingmar Johansson (recent World Heavyweight Boxing Champion) was then contracted to be at a game to sign autographs and pose with fans for pictures. When Short arrived at the stadium he was pleased to see the long line of fans waiting near the entrance. As it turned out they were there only to witness the famous world champion boxer as he entered the arena. It seemed that the only way to increase attendance would be to have a winning team.

There had been talk in 1957 about selling the franchise to another city. Short signed Elgin Baylor as number one in the NBA draft in 1958—Baylor was willing to skip his senior year at Seattle University. Baylor was a gifted shooter, a strong rebounder and accomplished passer. He dazzled spectators with his acrobatic jumping and his spectacular hook shot. Short said, "If he had turned me down then, I would have been out of business. The club would have gone bankrupt."

Early in 1960, Short took Jerry West as the second overall pick in the NBA. West—who the team nicknamed "Clutch"— helped the team return to the playoffs, averaging thirty points a game. Later in 1960 the team moved to Los Angeles, where West made the All-Star team fourteen times and set a scoring record for the Lakers.

## The Douglas DC-3

The Douglas DC-3 is a fixed-wing, propeller-driven aircraft that caused a revolution of air transport in the 1930s and 1940s, and is generally regarded as one of the most significant transport aircraft ever made.

The DC-3 was engineered by a team led by chief engineer Arthur E. Raymond, and first flew on December 17, 1935 (the 32nd anniversary of the Wright Brothers flight at Kitty Hawk). The plane was the result of a marathon phone call from American Airlines CEO C.R. Smith demanding improvements in the design of the DC-2. The amenities of the DC-3 (including sleeping berths on early models and an in-flight kitchen) popularized air travel in the United States. With just one refueling stop, transcontinental flights across America became possible. Before the DC-3, such a trip would entail short hops in commuter aircraft during the day coupled with train travel overnight.

Early airline companies like United, American, TWA, and Eastern ordered over 400 DC-3s. These fleets paved the way for the modern American air travel industry, quickly replacing trains as the favored means of long distance travel across the United States. During World War II, many civilian DC-3s were drafted for the war effort and thousands of military versions of the DC-3 were built under the designations C-47, C-53, R4D, and Dakota. The armed forces of many countries used the DC-3 and its military variants for the transport of troops, cargo, and wounded. In all, over 10,000 aircraft were produced.

\* \* \* \* \*

When examining a map of the U.S. and noting the location of the other seven NBA franchises, it was apparent that the Lakers had a costly transportation problem. Most of the teams were located in the East where they could easily travel by train or bus. That was not practical for the Minneapolis team. In order to overcome this problem, team owner Bob Short bought a former Airline DC-3 through Gopher Aviation. It was agreed that Gopher Aviation would provide pilot service and airplane maintenance.

The DC-3 no longer qualified under Part 121 of Federal Aviation Regulations to fly passengers as an airliner. The airplane would have to undergo a very costly modification consisting partly of upgrading the electrical system to accommodate the increased modern electrical demands. The airplane was qualified, however, to fly passengers under Part 91 of Federal Regulations as a private operator. All operators of private and personal aircraft were governed by these same regulations.

As a pilot employed by Gopher Aviation, I was assigned as co-pilot on the DC-3. I did not have a rating to fly as captain though I had been flying a much larger twin-engine airplane, the C-119 Flying Boxcar as captain and instructor with the active Air Force Reserve.

For most of the Lakers' 1959 season I had been flying as co-pilot with two different captains, Carl Taylor and Russ Reinhart. These two guys were very experienced, having flown many hours in the DC-3. I was fortunate to have had the opportunity to learn from them. They would allow me fly and even land the airplane at times.

We had flown to all the other seven cities in the league for games and, thanks to the players, I was able to attend many of the games. Once, when playing the New York Knickerbockers in Madison Square Garden, the guys had me carry an equipment bag into their locker room and then they invited me to sit by the bench with them. I had this opportunity at most stadiums. It was like being in a sports heaven watching the great players of that time—Wilt Chamberlain, Bob Cousy, Elgin Baylor, and the many other great players of that era.

In addition to flying as an air taxi pilot and co-pilot on the team's airplane, I had been flying with the Air Force Reserve. As a fighter pilot, I had recently flown the P-51 Mustang and the F-80 jet fighter for four years. During the past two and a half years, I had been flying the twin engine Fairchild C-119—I logged nearly 2,000 hours in that aircraft, most of it as first pilot and instructor pilot. This flying involved trips ranging from Alaska to Panama and all parts of the continent carrying cargo and troops. Every type of weather imaginable was commonplace on these flights.

On January 16, 1960, I was assigned to fly as co-pilot on a trip to St. Louis with Verne Ullman as captain and Jim Holznagel, a trainee who was learning to co-pilot the DC-3.

\* \* \* \* \*

### Jim Holznagel, Co-Pilot in Training

Jim and I are kindred spirits—we have a special bond. We each credit the other for saving his life, but in reality it was teamwork that allowed us to enjoy many more years of awesome flying adventures.

Jim left Gopher Aviation not long after the cornfield landing and flew with airlines for four years, and then flew for corporations on various airplanes including jets for ten years. Jim flew as a bush pilot and transport pilot for Alaska International Air, Great Northern Air, and Wright Air Services, alternating between bush flying and worldwide transport in the stretched version of the Lockheed C-130. Jim has since retired after forty-three years as a pilot having accumulated 26,200 flying hours without an accident.

The passage below is one of Jim's favorite bush flying stories.

### *Lucky the Skydiver,* by Jim Holznagel

A number of years ago, while flying for Wright Air Service, I had a trip up to Squaw Lake, Alaska in the Brooks Range. It was early spring, around mid-April. A man and his wife wanted to be dropped off on the east end of the lake where there was an old trapper's cabin built back in the early 1900s by a gold miner. That miner was the grandfather of the wife on this trip. She and her husband had come up from Portland, Oregon to follow in her grandfather's footsteps and do a little gold mining.

We were flying the C-185 on skis loaded down with what they figured they would need for equipment, grub, and whatever. They also had with them a little black pup about eight weeks old.

Prior to departure we talked about their plans and what we knew about that cabin. It was in pretty bad shape and needed some work for sure. Their plan called for being re-supplied as soon as the ice was out and I could get in on floats.

We left Fairbanks for Squaw Lake and upon our arrival we found the cabin much like I had described it. Being a young and energetic couple, they believed that it would pose no big problems and I left them there.

As time went by, around the first part of June, we received a call from some of their family members in Portland stating that they wanted to go along with me when I went to re-supply them and visit them for a short time.

We left Fairbanks in the float-equipped C-209 on the planned day, loaded with the two visiting family members and a large supply of food for them. As we arrived at Squaw Lake, we found the two miners and another couple waiting for us. Tom and Vi Goggins were their nearest neighbors living ten or so miles to the east. The two couples had met recently by accident. As we taxied to shore we could see them in the distance waving and laughing with joy, no doubt, very happy to see us.

The miners had enough and wanted out. Gold mining was not what they had expected it to be. They gave all the food and supplies we had brought to Tom and Vi as well as the little dog that was now five or six months old. We loaded all their gear and after a goodbye to Tom and Vi we taxied out for takeoff. Not to be left behind as his family departed without him, the little dog jumped aboard our airplane on one of the floats.

Tom Goggins told the next part of the story to me several months later when I returned to Squaw Lake. The little dog hunkered down for dear life as we began to take off. No one on the airplane was aware of him being onboard the float and away we all went for Fairbanks. When we were about one hundred feet in the air, the little dog bailed out and landed in the water near the far end of the lake. No worse for the wear, he swam to shore and teamed up with his new family, Tom and Vi.

The next winter, 'Old Lucky' showed up at Bob Akemann's cabin on Chandalar Lake some fifteen or twenty miles from the Goggins place, looking as though he had tangled with a moose or some other critter. On my next trip to Chandalar Lake, he climbed onboard with me as I was leaving, so I took him home to his real family. As they were reunited there was much joyous tail-wagging and petting and they were a family again.

## Jim Krebs

After his senior season at SMU, Krebs was selected by the Minneapolis Lakers with the third overall pick in the 1957 NBA draft. He played with the Lakers for seven seasons. His statistically strongest season occurred in 1961-62 when he averaged 10.0 points and 7.9 rebounds.

Jim Krebs was known in the league as man who was willing to go beyond the rules in getting his man. Though he could be aggressive on the court, teammates described Krebs as fun-loving and charismatic. A *Los Angeles Times* sportswriter wrote, "Time and again I've seen him make a team that was about to cry, laugh." Jim was often seen with his Ouija board and at one time predicted his age at death to be thirty-three. He later died at age twenty-nine from a freak accident while helping a neighbor clear a half-fallen tree.

# 4

# "CEILING AND VISIBILITY UNLIMITED"

*Saturday, January 16, 1960. Minneapolis, Minnesota*

The Douglas DC-3 had been pulled from the Gopher Aviation hangar at Fleming Field in South St. Paul, fueled and inspected prior to departure. We then flew to the Minneapolis airport (MSP) and taxied to north De Ponti Aviation to pick up our passengers. The destination of this flight was Lambert Field, St. Louis, Missouri, where the Minneapolis Lakers were scheduled to play the St. Louis Hawks on Sunday. Vernon Ullman, a former Navy pilot and war veteran, was assigned as first pilot. I had been flying as co-pilot on the Doug for most of the 1959-1960 NBA season and this was my first trip as co-pilot with Verne. Jim Holznagel, an outstanding young air taxi pilot was in the jump seat for orientation and training prior becoming co-pilot after meeting the necessary qualifications.

The airplane was stocked with soft drinks, reading material, and snacks. The passengers began to arrive and placed their luggage near the cargo door. When everyone was present, Jim and I loaded the luggage and basketball equipment bags, placing the heaviest items forward and the lightest to the rear to conform to proper weight and balance limits.

After checking the in-flight and destination weather, I had filed an instrument flight plan to Lambert Field St. Louis on Victor Airways for 9,000 feet altitude. The weather was clear with nothing to be concerned about. We would have a quartering tail wind for most of the route changing to a slight headwind further south. Our flight time was estimated to be three hours and ten minutes.

In addition to the three pilots, we boarded twenty passengers, including team coach, Jim Pollard, his 11-year-old son, Jack, and players Elgin Baylor, Tommy Hawkins, Dick Garmaker, Boo Ellis, Bob Leonard, Rod Hundley, Frank Selvy, Jim Krebs, and Larry Faust. The others were ten men, women, and children who were associated with team ownership and management: Frank Ryan, attorney, team secretary and treasurer, and his wife Virginia; team physician Dr. Bofenkamp and his wife Kathy; Eva Ullman, pilot Verne's wife; and Mr. French with his wife and two children.

We were all loaded and ready to start the engines. Looking out the co-pilot's window, I motioned to the fireguard, with my forefinger pointing up and circling. This told him that we were ready to crank and to guard against anyone walking into the propeller. With the APU (Auxiliary Power Unit) plugged in and online, Verne began to crank engine one. After a few puffs of smoke the engine coughed and began to purr. The fireguard moved around to engine two and soon it also was running smoothly.

I flipped on the radio, selected proper radio frequency and called clearance delivery for our flight clearance. The tower responded, "Are you ready to copy?" After receiving the clearance, I read it back including the proper departure procedure and called ground control for taxi clearance.

"You are cleared to taxi to runway 29 right; follow the taxiway in front of you past the tower and await further instructions." We were soon in the run-up spot for Runway 29 Right. We completed the before-takeoff checklist with magneto check and engine run-up complete and we were ready to go. I told the tower we were ready, and after holding position until landing aircraft had cleared the runway, the tower came over the radio: "Lakers DC-3, you are cleared for takeoff, with a straight-out departure. Contact departure control when airborne."

Verne advanced the throttles smoothly and set the takeoff power. I called out the airspeed, and nearing ninety knots Verne eased back on the control column and we were airborne and on our way. Verne called "gear up" and I raised the gear handle. The grinding sound of the gear retracting followed by two green lights indicated the gear was up and locked into position. Verne asked me to set METO power (Maximum Except Take Off), also known as climb power, with the throttles and called "flaps up." I raised the flap handle and checked the flap indicator for zero degrees.

After entering the takeoff time in the flight log, I selected the radio frequency for Departure Control and called for instructions. There was not much traffic and we were cleared to climb to 9,000 feet on course and contact Minneapolis control center on assigned frequency for flight monitoring and reporting. After leveling at 9,000 feet, Minneapolis Center, with the aid of radar, clocked us with a ground speed of nearly 200 knots, indicating a good tailwind.

Looking down from nearly two miles up, I noticed that the white blanket of snow was melting. The countryside was colored with various shades of brown, white and black, with water standing in the low spots from the melting snow. Judging from the large amounts of water in the fields, it was apparent that the farmers would have a problem in the spring. From a pilot's point of view, however, the weather on this day was ideal and was often called CAVU (Ceiling And Visibility Unlimited). Our entire route of flight was dominated by a high pressure area.

Jim and I knew from our weather briefing for today's flight that a low pressure area was approaching from the northwest. This condition could cause trouble for our return flight. If the high pressure area were to stall out over the southeast and the low pressure move in over the southwest, some very bad weather could develop. When side by side, the two systems could form a pumping action due to the counterclockwise rotation of the low pressure area and the clockwise rotation of the high pressure area. This action could bring a flow of warm moist air from the Gulf of Mexico, and when this air collides with the frigid arctic air from the north, all hell could break loose for pilots flying in the area.

As we passed Cedar Rapids, Iowa, I was instructed to contact Kansas City Center, and soon we were handed over to St. Louis Approach Control. I called Youngs Aviation on the Unicom frequency and gave them our estimated time of arrival and requested four cabs for the passengers. We listened to the St. Louis ATIS (Automatic Terminal Information Service) and learned that the weather was clear with wind out of the northwest at 12 to 15 MPH; our current altimeter setting was 29.89.

Lambert approach control came over the radio. "Lakers flight is cleared to descend to three thousand feet; contact Lambert tower ten miles out; no traffic in sight."

"Lambert tower, Lakers DC-3 requests landing instructions."

"Enter left, downwind for runway 30 and call on final." After touchdown, the tower instructed us to contact ground control for taxi instructions, and ground control directed us to Young's Aviation, the main fixed base operator, located on the southwest corner of the airport.

We were met by a follow-me jeep and led to our parking spot where the taxicabs were waiting. With those reliable engines shut down, Verne climbed out of the cockpit and de-planed with the others after Jim opened the door and helped the passengers out. I double-checked that all switches were turned off and then filled out the flight log and locked the flight controls. When the wheel chocks were in place, I released the brakes, climbed out of my seat and joined Jim who was helping off-load the luggage. The passengers grabbed their bags, loaded the cabs, and headed to downtown St. Louis for a Saturday night on the town. As the cabs pulled away, I asked Jim if Verne had given him a number where he could be reached. Jim shook his head, saying, "They were in a big hurry to get going."

Jim and I checked in with the FBO (fixed base operator) and then went to the nearby flight service station to check the weather expected overnight and the next day. "Now I know what that tail-wind was all about," Jim remarked. "A good old snowstorm could be moving across the Midwest and the plains from the Canadian pacific region."

St. Louis was predicting light rain beginning near morning with temperatures dropping. With the weather outlook, I decided we should get our bird in a hangar until departure the next day. We had to hang around another two hours for the ground crew to arrange hangar space, but once the Doug was squeezed into a hangar spot for the night, we checked for motel accommodations. A nearby motel had room and would send their courtesy van to pick us up in half an hour—a benefit for aircrews.

After unpacking our overnight bags in our adjoining rooms, Jim and I were not too tired to have a few beers in the motel bar. For pilots this was a favorite time of relaxation and hangar flying, with plenty of adventure story swapping. After a good steak dinner in the motel café we were ready to call it a day. We sat around my room for a short time talking about the weather forecast and soon Jim said, "I think I'll hit the sack, Giff. Tomorrow could be a long day."

"You could be right, Jim, I'm about ready for some shut-eye, too." I was rather exhausted, having been logging long hours between the Air Force Reserve, air taxi flights and the Lakers. I snagged a Nut Goodie candy bar from my flight bag and turned on the TV. The weather report confirmed what Jim and I had learned earlier. The winter storm was gaining momentum and St. Louis was expecting near freezing temperatures with low ceilings and light rain for later in the day.

# 5

# ENVELOPED IN DARKNESS

*Sunday, January 17, 1960, St. Louis, Missouri*

In the morning, a mid-winter storm was blowing down from the northwest with heavy snow and high winds across the plains. Opening the blinds revealed a hazy grey daylight with a bleak scene and a slight drizzle. Temperatures were well above freezing but dropping and it didn't look like a very good day for flying.

After a shower and a shave, I got dressed and found Jim ready to roll. As we enjoyed a leisurely breakfast in the motel café, Jim read the morning paper he had picked up from a nearby booth, glancing at the weather map.

Having had flown in this part of the country for several years, I was quite familiar with the somewhat unpredictable weather patterns. We were presently in an area on the map known as the "golden triangle," a triangle formed by Kansas City, Minneapolis and Chicago. Within this triangle, the warm moist gulf air would collide with the cold arctic air and create violent thunderstorms, beginning in the spring. The "golden" name referred to the fiery lightning in these thunderstorms. In winter, this meeting of air masses often resulted in a big mess for pilots with snow and ice. Higher performance pressurized airplanes could fly above the storms, but the unpressurized aircraft were committed to the lower levels where the bad stuff was.

After lounging around and discussing our plan of attack, we decided to pack our bags and check out. I placed a call to Youngs Aviation for crew transport, and soon we were at the airport checking our airplane for servicing with fuel, oil and interior detailing. Satisfied that our bird was ready for action, we checked in at the weather station and began monitoring the storm's movement.

The Lakers were playing the Hawks and were scheduled to fly to Minneapolis later in the day, but as the day passed, the weather appeared more foreboding. We checked PIREPS (pilot reports) and found out that pilots were experiencing heavy icing in the clouds north of St. Louis with worsening ground conditions.

I had been stationed at Jefferson Barracks just across the river for basic training during the war, and I knew the local winter weather was very difficult to predict. At times these storm systems would be held back by a high-pressure area further southeast, but one never knew.

I decided to contact Verne to discuss my concern about the weather, mainly the possibility of an ice storm paralyzing ground as well as air travel and heavy icing aloft. I intended to suggest that he and the passengers not rush to the airport until checking with me. Filing a flight plan into an area of known heavy icing was against FAA rules in addition to being a bad choice. I knew our vintage aircraft was not ideally suited for extremely heavy IFR (flying on instruments only in very bad weather conditions).

Verne had checked out of the hotel along with the other passengers and I assumed they went to the game. I attempted to have him paged at the auditorium, but received no response. I hoped that as flight captain he had been following the weather and had already made a decision to cancel or at least delay the flight.

Having checked the latest available weather information, Jim and I returned to Young's Aviation. As we walked from the flight service station to the hangar, the darkening night with a light haze and a chilling mist heightened my concern. Again we checked for messages, but there were none. The temperature dropped to just above freezing with a light drizzle, and the increasing darkness made the sky appear more ominous.

Later, while walking around our airplane checking for fluid leaks and tire condition, we heard the sound of the huge hangar doors grinding open above the noise of the heater fan hanging from the ceiling. Out of the darkness appeared four yellow taxis with Verne and the luggage, which was deposited in the hangar. The team and passengers had been dropped off at the terminal café for dinner. Verne asked, "Have you filed a flight plan?"

"No, I've been waiting to hear from you. I'm worried about the pilot reports of heavy icing for much of our route."

Without replying, he turned away, picked up the flight service phone and filed an IFR (Instrument Flight Rules) flight plan after receiving a brief update on the destination weather. "Let's load up the luggage and get ready. We have to pick up our passengers at the terminal when they call here," he said.

The situation had developed into what pilots call "get home-itis." Considering the cost of overnight hotel accommodations and the additional expenses involved for all, it became a factor in decision-making though it definitely should not have been. I suggested sweating it out for a few hours before deciding to depart. Soon, a phone call came from the passengers telling us they were finished dining at the terminal and were ready.

There was a slight delay in getting a tug to pull us out, so we turned on the interior lights while stowing the luggage. The tug arrived, but the crew did not have the correct tow bar, resulting in a further delay. When our airplane was finally pulled outside, the light rain pelting the shiny metal of aircraft showed signs of light ice particles. An attempt to start the engines with battery power was futile as the batteries were by now very low. An auxiliary power unit was plugged in and the ground crew had difficulty getting its engine going, but before long we had power. As the ground crew stood by with the fire extinguisher, I completed the before-starting-engines checklist.

"Clear number one!" Verne called as the prop began turning and the engine coughed with a belch of smoke and came alive with a soft rumble. With number two started, I turned on the generators and both of them came online. I noticed a high amperage draw as the generators were charging the nearly depleted batteries. I signaled the ground crew to disconnect the external power. The interior lights brightened and I turned on the radio to call ground control for clearance to taxi to the terminal for passenger pickup. We taxied to the transient passenger gate and parked. As the passengers began to appear, Verne cut the left engine as Jim opened the door to board everyone. Jim gave the passengers the normal briefing and checked that all seat belts were fastened. Jim cautioned the players about using the electric cup for heating soup and chili without checking with him; this appliance caused a very heavy amperage draw when used.

I called clearance delivery to receive our flight clearance and the response was, "You are cleared to MSP (Minneapolis Airport) via flight plan route with a straight out departure." I read it back and we were handed over to ground control and cleared to taxi to runway 30. On the run-up pad we checked the magnetos and completed the before-takeoff checklist.

"Lambert tower, this is Lakers DC-3, ready for takeoff." The Minneapolis Lakers DC-3, loaded with twenty-three souls was cleared for takeoff on runway 30.

It was eight in the evening and the weather was rather marginal with 300-foot ceiling and three quarters of a mile visibility. Because of the temperature and moisture, I flipped the pitot heater switches on to prevent icing of the air induction tubes that provided ram air for the airspeed indicators.

Verne applied takeoff power as I backed him up with the throttles. I monitored the airspeed, and when calling out ninety knots Verne eased back on the control column. We were airborne and I raised the gear and flaps on Verne's command and helped to set climb power. Shining my flashlight on the windscreen, I detected light ice forming. Lambert tower cleared us to climb to 8,000 feet on course and to contact departure control on the assigned frequency.

As we climbed, we flew on instruments in a very dark and ominous sky. During the climb in these conditions it was customary to flick on the right landing light to check for ice buildup and determine if the de-icing boots should be activated. I depressed the mike button to respond to tower's instructions. Instantly the radio faded, decreasing in volume until there was total silence. Simultaneously, the lights on the panel dimmed and flashed bright, and then went totally dark. The entire aircraft was now enveloped in darkness.

# 6

# NAVIGATING BY THE NORTH STAR

We were still in the clouds flying on instruments. I knew that we would soon be on top in the clear and we would be able to better evaluate our situation. Pilots always had a flashlight near at hand while flying at night; I had one on my lap and turned it on, handing it to Jim in the jump seat to check the panel. I realized that we were in big trouble, though it was reassuring to hear the engines still purring away with a powerful drone.

In a situation like this with the airplane trimmed for climb, a pilot could release the controls momentarily and continue the climb hands off. Both amp meters were pegged out at zero as well as the fuel gauges and all other electrical gauges. We had lost both generators and the ship's batteries were drained. With this old electrical system, no emergency procedure existed except to fly the airplane with what we had and find a safe place to land as soon as possible.

Of equal or greater concern was my observation that Verne had not been responding to the emergency. Normally in a situation such as this, the captain would become assertive in some manner dictating what we should be doing, but Verne had reached up and turned off the battery switch—perhaps in hopes that would be of some help—and then he just sat there in silence. The controls had been trimmed for climb and I said, "I'll take it, Verne," as he released the column and I continued the climb.

In many ways, we were in the same situation as U.S. Airmail pilots of the past when radios and navigational aids were non-existent. The following paragraph was eloquently expressed by Ernest K. Gann on page two of the preface in his book, *The Aviator*.

> They wound their way in good weather and bad by employing a combination of experience, daring and cunning. They found within themselves a sort of sixth sense of chance and direction because they had to.

Once launched into the sky they simply disappeared, as we had from the traffic controllers. After a certain amount of time they reappeared without ceremony and without anyone on earth knowing of their interim whereabouts. Sometimes they did not reappear. Under these circumstances, I was confident that I would be able to find a way to reappear. Many hours of simulator training had taught me that staying calm would give me a clearer mind and a much better chance of survival.

After leveling out on top of the cloud layer, we were at eight thousand feet altitude. We were delighted to see that we still had a vacuum-driven artificial horizon, which is used to keep the wings level and determine aircraft nose up or down attitude while flying on instruments only. Thank God the engineers at Douglas Aircraft came up with this system, as without it we would have really been up a creek. The magnetic compass was helpful (provided a pilot knew of its peculiarities). We had an airspeed indicator as long as we stayed out of icing; the heated air induction tube for airspeed indication would not function without electric power. The turn indicator was vacuum-powered and its needle pivoted like a wagging finger to show rate of turn. A small ball enclosed in an elliptical trace like a carpenter's level helped to make a coordinated turn without slipping. We were back to basic instrument flight, which had been drilled into us in the old Link Trainer during military training years ago—the old needle ball and airspeed method.

The C-119 I had been flying was much newer and larger, with a more sophisticated electrical system. It had generator failure warning lights and current limiters but the old Doug had none of these. With the first sign of generator trouble the procedure was to turn off all unnecessary equipment including the bad generator and battery, and to use equipment sparingly to avoid overloading the good generator.

I thought of the many hours in the C-119 flight simulator when the instructor operating it tried his best to cause me to crash. I learned to keep my cool during crises in order to think clearly and above all, to fly the airplane.

The darkened cockpit became very quiet; there was no doubt about the seriousness of our present situation. Jim and I had spent most the day at the weather station and we had a pretty good idea of what to expect. North of Des Moines, it was forecast to be improving as the front moved south. Having thoroughly checked the weather, I was able to suggest a plan of action that Verne agreed with. After breaking out on top, I suggested we head north using the North Star, hoping to stay on top of the storm, reach the improving weather and continue on to Minneapolis.

We would then use basic visual means to navigate. If we were to reach an area where we could see the ground it would have been a simple matter to head for a town and check the name on their lighted water tower. The bright lights of the many small towns in the area would make it easy to find them, and provide a clue as to our location.

Meanwhile the operators in the control tower and departure control at St. Louis, having lost radio contact with us, were scratching their heads trying to figure out just what we were up to. I had thought about trying the old recommended procedure to fly left triangles with one minute legs indicating no radios but decided that would entail too many uncertainties besides unnecessary fuel burning. We were confident that we could navigate with the North Star and get over the storm to better weather.

At this time I used an old procedure for saving fuel in a crisis. This involved leaning the carburetor and air mixture until the engine backfired, and then advancing the power ten revolutions per minute.

It seemed rather simple to follow my plan and—no sweat—all would end well. Coach Pollard was closely monitoring the cockpit activity and I assumed our apparent confidence was relieving his concerns for the safety of all passengers. Verne had instructed Jim to inform the passengers of the nature of our problem and how we intended to handle it.

Since the cabin was totally without heat or lights, the passengers were literally left in the dark. If we had a speaker system, I could imagine the captain saying, "This is your captain speaking; we are very sorry for the inconvenience of having to be without heat and lights but just bundle up, make yourselves comfortable, say a few prayers and enjoy the flight. Oh, by the way, we have just lost our electrical system, leaving us without radios for communication and navigation, but we hope to find a way to be safely on the ground in a few hours as soon as we find better weather and a suitable place to land."

As expected, we found the cloud tops to be around eight thousand feet. We were greeted with nature's awesome beauty as seen by pilots—a bright moon was shining on the billowing cloud tops beneath, appearing as millions of sheep huddling together as far as we could see. From above, myriads of glittering stars in the Milky Way peered down as sentinels of our universe. Enjoying and appreciating this spectacle seemed in a way like an answer to a prayer, inspiring confidence.

Charles Lindbergh was once asked what he liked about flying, and one of his answers was the beauty. The majestic beauty of this night might have been what he had in mind. A pilot's view of the many sights is awesome. There were times when it was like having the best seat in the house, viewing "The Theater Of Seasons" accompanied by the roar of Wright Cyclone Engine Duet and the Humming Propellers.

It was terribly cold, probably in the teens. We were shivering but keeping busy so we didn't worry about the cold. I was lucky to be wearing a heavy wool tweed suit that I had purchased recently while in Bermuda on an Air Force mission. Our passengers must have been freezing cold. Tommy Hawkins, a rookie, was sitting in the rear with Bob Leonard and asked if Bob thought they'd make it. Bob responded, "Sure, Tommy, these pilots are both WW II vets with lots of flying experience and they're good, so don't worry." Jim Krebs sat with his Ouija board on his lap, illuminated by a penlight, trying to predict the outcome of our situation. Others were bargaining with God, hoping for His help. There was no doubt that the passengers were extremely worried— I know that I would have been if I were back there with them.

I sure could've used one those flying suits I wore on my first solo flight in November 1943. It was of soft brown leather lined with thick sheep's wool, complete with boots and a helmet with goggles. I really needed that outfit in North Texas during mid-winter.

Verne seemed to be satisfied with my plan as we pressed on in a northerly direction. We had continued flying with the North Star visible in the windscreen and our plan seemed to be working. It became necessary to climb higher and higher to top the ice-filled storm clouds. I asked Jim, "Do you remember checking for cloud tops in the area?"

"No, it didn't seem relevant at the time." It sure would have been good to know just how high we had to climb to top these suckers. Climbing to 15,000 feet in our present situation, without oxygen, was at the moment of no great concern.

As a military pilot flying pressurized aircraft, I was required to attend physiological training every three years. Part of this training was conducted in an altitude chamber, where with simulated high altitudes I was able to detect symptoms of hypoxia—brain impairment due to a lack of oxygen. On one occasion this training was life-saving.

I was flying alone in an Air Force P-80 jet fighter from Minneapolis to Tinker AFB (Air Force Base), Oklahoma for a parts pick-up. While rapidly climbing through 26,000 feet, I began to feel strange and decided to make an entry in my flight progress log when I dropped my pencil. While lowering my head nearly between my knees to recover the pencil I began experiencing massive "floaters" blurring my sight. While inhaling with my gaze focused on the oxygen blinker (a watch-sized dial which blinked like an eye with each drawn breath of oxygen), I realized it was inoperative. Simultaneously, I rolled the nose trim down, retarded the throttle and deployed the dive boards. Upon reaching a lower altitude, I could breathe normally again. I had been near the point of becoming unconscious, and this all occurred in a matter of seconds. Had I not realized my oxygen hose was not connected and detected my hypoxia at 26,000 feet, I would have very soon been unconscious and the jet would have continued to climb as high as it could before running out of fuel—and that would have been a disaster. It was a lesson learned and would never happen again.

On the way home from Tinker, I found the North Star, placed it in the center of the windscreen, and knew that in about forty-five minutes I would be able to look down and see the lights of Minneapolis and St. Paul.

\* \* \* \* \*

### The Card Table

On the long flights to and from the East coast, the players stacked suitcases in the aisle of the airplane, making a card table to engage in another competition. Coach Pollard's wife, Arilee, decided to make a card table that fit over the arm rests, covering it with red felt like that of a casino blackjack table.

After the reunion in 1960, I received a message from Arilee, who lives in Lodi, California. She had found the card table in an attic and asked what should be done with it. I suggested that it go to the Carroll, Iowa historical museum. It was then delivered to Carroll where it is now on display and pictured below.

# 7

# FUEL CLOCK TICKING

We were now above 15,000 feet and finding it difficult to top the clouds. In mountain climbing from here up to 26,000 feet it is known as the dead man's curve. We had entered the clouds and began picking up ice. Our right engine was cutting in and out, due to carburetor ice and having leaned out the fuel mixture, I assumed. I advanced the mixture controls to full rich and attempted to apply carburetor heat but the lever wouldn't budge. Verne was OK with me at the controls and said nothing as the engine faltered. I made a hasty 180-degree turn and began a rapid descent trading altitude for airspeed in the event the backfiring engine didn't come back to normal. Just imagine the challenge I would face had the engine failed to come back to life. I desperately had to get out of this icing condition.

As we retreated from the storm we soon broke out in the clear on top and I was finally able to actuate the carburetor heat control. The engine coughed and sputtered a few times and came back to life with that reassuring roar. I was relieved knowing that we still had two good engines with which to find a way out of this mess.

Our brief encounter with heavy icing had left our windscreen heavily coated. Some ice had formed on the leading edges of the wings and engine nacelles. "Boy, we wouldn't have lasted long in that stuff; there would be nowhere to go but down," Jim said.

"Just imagine how we might have made out flying through this stuff at 8,000 feet on our original flight plan. A change of altitude may not have been an option due to conflicting traffic," I said. Perhaps fate was on our side causing us to shift using altitudes that experience had taught us would keep us out of serious trouble with ice.

Verne instructed Jim to find his luggage and bring his shaving kit to him. Verne took out two straight-edged blades and we each reached out attempting to scrape off the ice. We weren't getting anywhere with this—the inside was frosted over from the moisture in everyone's breath.

Having had flown straight north bucking a strong headwind using Polaris as a guide, I figured we were rather far east and slightly south of Des Moines after having reversed our course. We leveled out at 10,000 feet on top of the clouds and our windscreen was still covered with ice. Now what? Perhaps if we flew west while keeping the storm to our right we may find a hole in the storm or lower cloud tops. After flying west long enough to sense that we should be nearly south of Des Moines, it became obvious that we needed to come up with a different plan.

Time had been fleeting and soon the clock would be ticking on our unknown remaining fuel quantity. Knowing the nature of these storms, I knew that at a lower altitude it would be too cold for icing with snow and low visibility near the surface. Hopefully when we were north of Des Moines, we'd find improving weather as had been forecast. This would require a bold and somewhat daring decision to begin a northbound rapid descent into the clouds through the icing to 4,500 feet with the hope of not picking up much ice. At the time I could think of no other reasonable option. The enveloping darkness, extreme cold and pressing urgency of our situation dictated that I do this.

I declared this decision to Verne and Jim. Verne obviously agreed with this decision, remaining silent, while Jim said, "I think it's a good idea. Go for it, Giff." I made a rapid descent, limiting our exposure to icing as we turned north into the ice-filled clouds. As a twin engine instructor pilot, I was accustomed to monitoring the actions of the guy in the left seat but now I was on my own. We used the altimeter setting I had remembered for Des Moines. We leveled off at 4,500 feet altitude. I was right—we were in snow with no icing.

Jim and I had spent most of the day at the weather station learning all we could about the weather for our route of flight. We were expecting improvement north of Des Moines. Pilot reports had been telling of heavy icing in the clouds above 6,000 feet. Calculating that we had been on a northerly heading long enough to be nearing Des Moines, we began watching for the glow of the city lights through the snow. Sure enough, we soon detected a very extensive bright glow through the snow that covered a large area. Knowing that there would be no other large city in the area, it reassured us, providing positive orientation and confidence in the next phase of our plan.

Being reasonably certain to be north of Des Moines, my main concern was a group of towers near Des Moines. For several years I had flown all around this area using a sectional chart to navigate. These charts had shown the location of the highest towers in the area. An altitude of 4,500 feet would give us a good safety margin; it was also the altitude required for westbound VFR (visual flight rules) traffic, an even numbered altitude plus 500 feet. This provided separation from traffic in the Des Moines area flying at four or five thousand feet.

We were still hoping to find improving weather soon, but we had no such luck. We later learned that the weather front had stalled out and become an occluded front backing up far into Minnesota. Having no way of determining our fuel state, this became a matter of serious concern and that clock started ticking. Under normal conditions, we carried enough fuel for six hours and if we found no break in the weather, we were committed to go down and search for ground contact hoping to then find an airport or a suitable place to land.

This plan, though seeming to be bold, was really our only choice of action. The last situation we wanted was to run out of fuel and be committed to glide to a dead stick landing through the snow and clouds, landing or crashing wherever we happened to be. The odds of making it under those circumstances were very slim.

Verne broke his silence by suggesting we should continue on in the clouds, hoping to find better weather. In my opinion, this was a foolish gamble and in no way a good idea. If we were to lose an engine from fuel starvation after making visual contact with the ground, we could choose our crash site if necessary. It was now past one in the morning and we had been in the air over five hours. I knew if we ran the fuel tank too low there could be moisture or sediment in the tank bottom causing a problem. The threat of fuel starvation was a reality. I thought our odds were better cautiously searching for the bottom of the storm clouds. This was a rather daring plan, and Verne agreed with it. No other option made any sense to me. Being familiar with the area, I believed we were in level terrain. The highest obstructions near the surface would be windmills and farm silos.

I suggested making a very gradual descent on a north heading with a very good chance of safely establishing visual contact with the ground. Even if ground visibility was as low as an eighth of a mile obscured that would be around six hundred feet altitude where we would be able to see something below. I was reasonably certain of our location being northwest of Des Moines, and I knew from flying in this area that it was pretty flat and level terrain below. We definitely couldn't be so far west to have to worry about the Missouri River Bluffs.

We had to act soon—there was no other reasonable choice. I had not been much into prayer; I considered myself too insignificant in the eyes of a higher power to deserve intervention. But in these trying times, not only my life was in jeopardy but also the lives of twenty-two other men, women and children. I made a mental declaration to clean up my act and devote my life to helping others. Somehow my confidence was enhanced and I chose to implement my plan. Sometimes confidence is a matter of rearranging reality to suit my liking.

I began a gradual descent at the rate of 300 feet per minute as Jim shined his flashlight on the altimeter and rate of descent indicator. While I was looking down through the open weather window, Jim called out our altitude and monitored our rate of descent. "If we have the correct altimeter setting we are approaching 1,000 feet above the ground," Jim said. I decided to reduce our rate of descent to between 100 and 200 feet per minute and the airspeed to 120 knots.

Straining my eyes in the snowy void searching for sight of the ground, all I could see was an eerie blur when suddenly Jim tapped my shoulder and said, "We should be about 600 feet above the ground." Wow! We were right on as I began seeing ground lights here and there through the blowing snow. Soon blurry images of barns and silos appeared. I started to ease down a little more keeping a close eye out for anything ahead and flew with all the caution I could muster. As I eased the plane slightly lower our forward visibility became slightly improved, though snow was drifting across the ground. We were so close to the ground that I could make out farm fences with snow swirling through them. We needed to find a flat place to land and walk away from this nightmare. In the back of my mind, I was doing some bargaining with God.

Suddenly a blacktop road appeared beneath us, which I began to follow. Now we had a navigation aid—this road had to lead to a city or a town with a water tower and the town name printed on it. I was still flying the airplane with the road down and slightly to the right, clearly visible through my little side weather window. It wasn't necessary to hold my head out the window; that would have frozen my face badly. The window was situated so that it was possible to see down and slightly ahead. Cold air was moving through the cockpit chilling us, but nothing intolerable.

One of the Lakers players later remarked there was a lot of bargaining with God going on. Perhaps our lucky break in finding that highway had something to do with their bargaining. If pilots ever were in a desperate need of some form of a navigation aid it was then. A very large lighted Hamm's beer sign appeared on the right, with the dancing bear and the words "from the land of sky blue waters," a good indication that we were near Minnesota and approaching somewhere that this beverage was sold— another navigation aid probably provided from the praying that had been going on in the cabin. I had even muttered under my breath, "If anyone is listening or watching, we sure could use a little more help here."

Dick Garmaker, who had sold insurance in the off-season, was accused by other players of selling life insurance policies and after signing throwing them out the pilot's window. I disclaimed this in Dick's defense because nothing had been tossed out my window.

As I strained to follow the blacktop road I noticed wooded areas with drifting and blowing snow. I began reciting to myself the words from a Robert Frost poem I knew: "The woods are lovely, dark and deep, but I have promises to keep, and miles to go before I sleep." The promises to keep in the poem could have been those made as I had been bargaining with God.

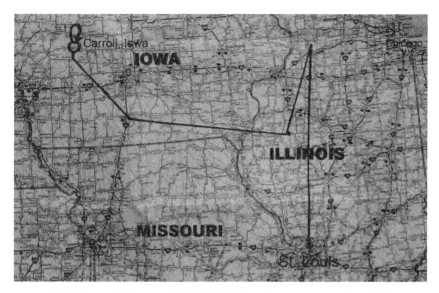

Estimated Route of DC-3 Flight, January 17-18, 1960

Following the North Star from St. Louis, we would have flown a straight line on a heading of true north and at a likely point northeast of Moline, Illinois, we were unable to stay on top of the clouds and turned south. Due to an unreliable magnetic compass from here on we likely had flown slightly southwest, attempting to head south for approximately seventy-five miles to somewhere southwest of Peoria, Illinois.

At this time we were on top of the clouds and in the clear at ten thousand feet altitude. From here we had flown approximately two hundred miles west by the compass near Osceola, Iowa. It was at this point that I had assumed we had to be somewhere south of Des Moines, Iowa, and had turned to a north heading on the fickle magnetic compass but likely tracked northwest. It was at this point that I had decided to descend through the ice-laden clouds to forty-five hundred feet.

After about a half hour on this heading we spotted the large area of brightness through the snow and believed that to be Des Moines. After leaving those lights behind and to our right I decided to go down to look for ground contact. At approximately fifty miles beyond the lights we were able to establish ground contact and soon thereafter we intercepted Highway 71 North and found Carroll, Iowa. From this point with all the circling and foolishness we were about half an hour in the air until finally landing five hours and forty minutes after leaving St. Louis.

I know that some pilots are going to measure the approximate distance traveled and say the math doesn't add up as the normal cruise speed of the DC-3 is 185 MPH and the approximate distance traveled was about six hundred and fifty miles. Based on these figures we would have been airborne for four hours at the most. Consider this: soon after breaking out on top, not long after takeoff, I had implemented my cruise control experience as Aircraft Performance Engineer in the South Pacific on a B-29 Bomber. I had leaned the carburetor fuel mixture and used a reduced power setting for what I considered to give us maximum endurance. Our overall ground speed had to be around 130 MPH after throwing in some pretty stiff headwinds. That's my story and I'm sticking to it.

# 8

# LIGHTS OF "LL"

I was right in my belief that this road had to lead to somewhere as a sight to behold appeared ahead. Looking out my weather window a large town with a water tower appeared. Those folks in the cabin must have been doing some powerful bargaining as we now had a new navigation-aid. With this, my spirits and hope soared.

As we passed by the water tower, we were disappointed, not able to read the name of this town because all the letters were plastered with the blowing and swirling snow except the last two—"LL." Someone had spray-painted in large black letters, "Seniors '59" on the tower. Where in the world could this be?

As we circled the town it became obvious that many alert residents were aware of our problem on this stormy night at one o'clock in the morning. As our arcs widened hoping to find an airport beacon, I spotted an unpicked cornfield on the very edge of town. I wished that the passengers would keep up their prayers—someone among them must have had a lot of influence. We even had a windsock; we spotted a large smokestack near the cornfield and the wind was blowing right down the rows of unpicked corn perhaps twenty miles per hour or higher. This would have made near ideal landing conditions under those circumstances. I was able to get a very good look at the cornfield and it seemed to be at least a quarter of a section and at least a quarter of a mile in length.

We were faced with a moment of truth and another critical decision. I suggested putting the airplane down in that cornfield immediately. In my opinion it was really a no-brainer. I viewed it as being as close to a normal landing as we could have wanted, with plenty of help nearby.

As a small child I had ridden with my Dad on a cultivator after carrying a fruit jar of cold well water to him; I knew there was no way there could there have been boulders, ditches or any obstacles in that field from what I had observed. The cornfield was close enough to the town that it was partially illuminated. Our fuel state was critical—we had now been airborne well over five hours.

As we continued circling and looking for an airport beacon, it seemed the entire town came alive as more lights began brightening the stormy night. The brightness from the awakened people made the cornfield much more visible and inviting. There was absolutely no doubt in my mind that we could land safely there. What a great sight it was; a feeling of confidence and comfort came over me as these people certainly realized we had a serious problem. They were helpless to do anything for us but knowing there were people concerned for our safety was very encouraging. If we encountered any problem on landing, help would be near. We later learned that as they watched our darkened airplane, the police had asked them to turn on their yard lights. Many residents had prayed for us.

I again suggested putting the airplane down in the cornfield while we still had the engines running, but Verne insisted on following the blacktop road north hoping for an airport nearby or better weather. This didn't make a lot of sense to me; an airport runway would not have been plowed, any runway lights would have likely been covered with snow and no one would have been nearby to help. We were uncertain about remaining fuel—we might not get very far north, and then what? Without the lights of the city it would be very dark out there. If we were to land where people could see us they certainly would have come to our aid immediately if necessary.

Coach Pollard and Frank Ryan supported my decision to land in the cornfield and suggested that Verne listen to me, but Verne, as captain, was adamant in insisting that we proceed northbound on the blacktop road to look for an airport or improving weather.

My gut tightened with the thought of what we might be getting into, with unknown fuel status and direction. It was scary to leave what I believed to be a sure thing for the unknown. I became more frightened than I had been all night. I was at the controls flying with my head partially out the window. I should have become suspicious of Verne's state of mind—this decision made no sense whatsoever. A mutiny or rebellion could have caused dissention and arguing in the cockpit – and that thought kept me on course. I was in control of the airplane from the right seat and was doing my best to keep the road in sight, but it was difficult with the darkness and blowing snow.

Momentarily it seemed the cloud tops above the storm were lowering, allowing a bright moon to lend a pale, eerie glow to the countryside. I was flying barely one hundred feet above the ground to maintain forward visibility, leaving very little margin for error. The wind was swirling the snow on the ground and at times partially obscuring our forward visibility.

Suddenly the road disappeared from my view—it must have taken a turn. I believe Verne's situational awareness was in sync with mine when I said, "I've lost it. Do you have it?"

He replied, "OK, I've got it," apparently not realizing that I referred to the road and simply taking over the controls. Jim, riding in the jump seat with his flashlight on the altimeter and rate of climb and descent indicator loudly warned, "Pull up, pull up!"

I had been warming my ears and face while rubbing my strained and watering eyes. Quickly, I glanced out the small weather window and my heart jumped as I realized we were about to fly into a grove of trees with the right wing lowered. This was what pilots lived in fear of. The tree branches and limbs seemed to rush toward me. We were so close to crashing that the wingtip brushed the treetops. Instinctively I pulled back on the control column, leveled the wings and hit the power.

Jim later said that he figured we were goners. Those trees were so close that it reminded me of riding on a train with my head pressed against the window, seeing the ground rush up at me after crossing a bridge. My heart pounded rapidly, providing a fresh blast of adrenalin—then I found we were back in the soup. Luckily after executing a gradual coordinated right descending turn, I again had the ground in sight. I was so frightened by nearly crashing and losing our only navigation aid that I was now super wide-awake.

Fate was my enemy as I battled to survive, but I bounced back and got another chance. Just how I was able to do all this at 150 feet above the ground in a matter of seconds, in a raging snowstorm at one in the morning, was difficult to understand. Providence was on my side in this encounter, with that merciless enemy, fate.

Knowing that the road was not very far behind, I guessed at heading south since we had been going north before pulling up and turning back. As the magnetic compass settled down, it verified my heading as south, and the surveyor's section lines on the ground backed up the compass. Losing our only navigation aid and nearly crashing a few moments prior made finding the road seem hopeless, but it had to be back there. I simulated the old radio range approach—after flying over the station I would reverse course, do a procedure turn, and re-intercept the beam.

I lucked out again as the plan worked and I found that beautiful black ribbon of asphalt. Without a doubt it was going to be the cornfield if we could make it before running out of fuel. The time clock on the fuel was ticking loudly in my mind. While following the blacktop road back toward the mystery town, Verne suddenly realized the danger of fuel starvation and suggested landing on the road. As a former crop-duster pilot I had bad experiences with that idea even in daylight. Power lines and other obstructions were always difficult to see and a serious hazard. I strongly opposed the suggestion; Coach Pollard suggested again that Verne listen to me and find that cornfield.

Our fuel state was critical and we needed to land very soon or we would be in real trouble. Seeing the lights of the town again lifted my spirits. As we approached the mystery community of LL, we observed that it was totally brightened by practically all the city lights aglow. It seemed a welcoming party was awaiting our arrival, and I became excited about the idea. I spotted a fire truck flashing a spotlight in the air but I didn't have time to investigate as we were committed to land in the cornfield as soon as possible.

"There it is, just off to our left. I'll line us up and you take over and land," I told Verne. My greatest fear was fuel starvation, which would seriously complicate matters after coming this close to safety. A feeling of great anxiety gnawed at my gut; Verne expressed doubts about the length of the cornfield and the landing gear position. My suggestion was to drop gear and flaps and make a quick low pass to be certain of the field length. There was no further discussion about landing gear up or down; I dropped the landing gear. Landing with the gear up made no sense—it would be difficult to get out of the airplane. "Why damage the airplane and have to fill out an accident report for no reason," I firmly stated.

Jim went back and instructed the passengers to expect a possible rough landing. Jim found Elgin Baylor sitting in the rear with no seat belt on and instructed him to get behind a jump seat and cover his face with his coat. I had complete confidence in knowing what we were doing—we would pull this off safely. Verne took over the controls after the low pass and I held a light on the panel while looking out my side window to keep us lined up as Verne watched the airspeed and descent.

On the short final approach, I looked out my window and

said, "We're lined up, let her down now." Verne held a safe air-speed and I held the last dying light on the panel. The cabin was deathly quiet as we neared the ground.

As our wheels neared the snow-covered cornfield I said, "Cut the power, Verne." We heard the corn ears banging the aircraft belly and I was ready to hold the control column all the way back. If the airplane began to nose over I'd blast the throttles which would blow the tail down but that wasn't needed as we slowed to a stop and cut the engines. We later learned that our tail wheel snagged a strand of barbed wire separating two cornfields.

I sat quietly in the cockpit for a moment considering how fortunate I had just been, letting the adrenalin subside. By all accounts I should have been dead by now in a burned and still-smoldering wreckage in a grove of trees. I was totally exhausted physically and emotionally. During the encounter with fate there was no time to think of anything except how to survive it. At one point, when it appeared there was a slim chance of making it, the thought did come over me, "The folks at home are going to feel bad about this." As I sat recovering from the experience, I said a silent prayer to the one who had spared my life. Climbing out of the cockpit and exiting the airplane took some time. It seemed difficult to return to the reality of normal life after that experience.

## Jim Pollard

On the flight, Jim Pollard and Frank Ryan were almost like additional crew members—they both stayed close to the cockpit and in touch with us. Both of these guys were highly skilled people experts, feeding us with atta-boys and encouragement. Their calming presence, telling us they knew we would handle the situation and get them down safely, calmed us. Ultimately it was these two guys who got through to Verne that the cornfield was the way to go.

Pollard played for Stanford and was a key member of Stanford's 1942 championship team. During WW II, he starred in Coast Guard teams from Alameda to Honolulu. Following the war, Pollard played for the San Diego Dons and the Oakland Bittners, making four trips to Denver for AAU playoffs. In the NBA, Pollard was considered one of the best forwards in the 1940s and 1950s, and was known for his leaping ability—Pollard would occasionally dunk from the free throw line during warm-ups, earning him the nickname "The Kangaroo Kid."

Pollard coached the Minneapolis Lakers in 1960, and ended his career after eight seasons, beginning in the NBL in 1947. Pollard was considered an exceptional all-around athlete. During his NBA career, Pollard also played amateur baseball for Jordan, Minnesota's Town Team baseball club. He was reputed to be "a good pitcher and a powerful hitter." It was there that Pollard famously "hit a ball that didn't stop until it got to Chicago," because it landed in a gondola car in a freight train passing by the ballpark. Jim died at age 71 in 1973.

# 9

# NO BUSINESS FOR
# THE UNDERTAKER

Everyone on board realized we were safe on the ground and the silence was broken by the loudest cheering and shouting I could've imagined. With crew and passengers confined to the cabin, it sounded like a packed stadium. There was so much joyful emotion displayed by the thankful group that it created an almost electric feeling among us.

The only time I've experienced that was in 1987, sitting just above the third base line as the runner headed for home to win the World Series for the Minnesota Twins. The crowd of sixty-four thousand erupted in a vibrant display of joy and celebration with hugging, high-fiving and waving of homer hankies. This group seemed to be permeated with a similar electric-like sensation.

It was 1:40 AM, January 18, 1960—a date and time that would never be erased from the memories of all on board. There were twenty-three men, women and children, who for approximately five and a half hours, did not know if they were going to live or die in a horrible disaster. Some of the passengers thought of the unfortunate incident less than a year ago when Buddy Holly and the Big Bopper died not too far from our location in an airplane crash in a cornfield near Mason City, Iowa.

After unlocking the cabin door, Jim was the first out. I heaved a sigh of relief when my feet hit the snow. I survived the most challenging and harrowing flight of my entire career in aviation. An experience of this magnitude is permanently etched in one's memory in great detail—and all onboard could attest.

All others emerged joyfully from the tired and creaking old flying machine and were frolicking in the snow, making and throwing snowballs, hugging and high-fiving one another through tears and laughter. The flight crew received many hugs, back-slapping and high-fiving. It was then that "Hot Rod" Hundley had proclaimed his good fortune in living to love again.

I witnessed a great example of raw courage and maturity displayed by the players and other adults. Not for a moment during the perilous five hours and forty minutes had there been a sign of panic. Not once did anyone interfere with cockpit duties and activities. By their behavior, hope and confidence was instilled in all others, especially the children. In reality they were not too unlike someone on death row sweating out their last hours of life, thinking about how their death would affect loved ones. As for the flight crew, we had been totally occupied summoning all we had learned in training and experience to bring this flight to a satisfactory, safe conclusion.

The first to arrive and help us was a fire truck followed by a hearse. Among them was a local resident, Jim Herzog. Jim had been sleeping until he heard us buzzing around town. He quickly donned his clothing over his pajamas, and on the way out the door his wife asked what was he going to do. Jim had said, "I don't know, but those people up there are in trouble."

Our team plane in the middle of the Steffes cornfield (photos courtesy of the *Carroll Daily Times Herald*).

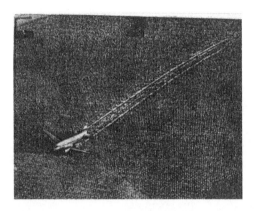

Two aerial photos of our aircraft taken later the day we landed. (Courtesy the *Carroll Daily Times Herald*)

As the many local residents made it through the snow to help, they supposed the hollering and loud noises were evidence of chaos and were expecting the worse—finding the dead and dying. Much to their surprise all were safe and still in a celebrating mood. Reportedly the hearse driver remarked to Tommy Hawkins, "I thought I was going to have some business tonight." Thank God that was not the case.

As the happy party went off to a nearby motor inn, Jim and I remained to put our tired old bird to bed, putting covers and control locks in place, and making certain that all switches were turned off and the windows up front were closed and the door locked. As we walked away, our reliable old bird's engines could be heard ticking and creaking as they cooled down after a long, hard workout. I slapped Jim on the back and said, "Jim, good buddy, the real hero of this adventure is now resting behind us. I can't think of any other bird that would have served us so well."

"I'll second that," he said.

An obliging gentleman was standing by to take us to the motel where the others had gone.

I was happy about being where we were instead of in a burning mess in that grove. We soon learned we were in Carroll, Iowa, which was not too far off course considering what we had to work with and the weather we had encountered. I was more concerned about being safe on the ground than where we were. The people of Carroll expressed their great relief in knowing that we were safe and genuinely made us feel welcome.

# 10

# "LIFE IS LIKE A MOUNTAIN RAILWAY"

I arrived at the Burke Motor Inn, briefly joining the others in their celebrating and waiting in line to phone home. There were no telephones in the room but phone booths were in the lobby. One of the players had a reputation for calling home after a few drinks with a wild excuse, and as he explained to his wife that we would be delayed, as we had to land in a cornfield in Iowa, she told him to call back when he was sober and hung up. Another player in line called the wife to confirm the story.

If there had been a bar in the hotel it would not have been open at two in the morning; however, there was a party room with a liquor cabinet but no one around with a key. One of the passengers knew how to open the lock and soon the happy group was engaged in some more serious celebrating. A note was left in the cabinet that the group would cover the cost of the spirits they drank. Someone handed me a glass half full of Old Fitzgerald and the first gulp really began to warm me through. With each sip it seemed as though all the nerves in my body were becoming untangled.

There had been some anxious moments at home. Someone had called my wife reporting that we were overdue and presumed down. My wife later learned we were safely on the ground after I was able to use a telephone.

An elderly man approached me and shook my hand, putting a big cigar in my breast pocket. His friendly demeanor and generosity was typical of the spirit of the people in Carroll. I told him to spread the word that the bright lights of the town and homes made it easier for us to land in that field. This action on the part of the townspeople had been a lifesaver and I'd never forget it.

After a brief chat, I thanked him, excused myself and went to my room. I slumped into a chair and lit the cigar, finishing off the bourbon as every sip began to take the chill out of my bones. I began trying to process what had happened. How fortunate we all were to be there in the motel among friendly hosts, safe, warm and comfortable. It was difficult for me to process just how close we all came to a horrible death. It nearly happened as a result of a foolish error in judgment and I wouldn't forget that.

I would always be thankful for the response of the people of Carroll, Iowa and the bright lights that helped us land safely. Nearly everyone in the town was pulling for us. I was grateful and would remember Carroll forever.

Jim came to the door and gave me a big hug. "Thanks, buddy, for being on the ball in that airplane and reacting to my warning. I thought for sure we were goners."

"Come in and sit down; I'm just beginning to unwind. How about you?" I said.

Jim replied, "My knees are still shaking from coming so close to buying the farm."

"I know a good cure for that." I led him to the liquor cabinet where the celebration continued. I found two glasses and a bottle of bourbon and poured a large amount for each of us. Back in my room, we clicked our glasses and toasted our teamwork and good fortune. We sat enjoying the warm and relaxing effect of the bourbon, trying to process what had happened. We both agreed that was about as close as we ever wanted to come to buying the farm. I felt the bourbon kicking in and said, "Jim, I feel so darn good that I feel like singing."

"You must be feeling that booze," he said, and then added, "What do you feel like singing, Giff?"

"'Life is Like a Mountain Railway,' do you know the words to it, Jim?"

"I sure do, but why did you pick that song? I thought you fighter pilots always sang 'The Whiffenpoof Song;' what the heck is a 'whiffenpoof,' anyway?" Jim asked.

"First, the name 'Whiffenpoof' originated in about 1910 in a comic opera, 'Little Nemo.' The Whiffenpoofs of Yale University represented the oldest college capello chorus in the U.S. From there the song became more famous, sung by Rudy Vallee in 1927 and Bing Crosby in 1947. It was also the background music in the movie 'Twelve O'Clock High,' in 1949 with Gregory Peck."

"Geeze, Giff, how come you know all that?"

"I've been asked that question many times, that's why," I mumbled through a bourbon-soaked breath. "Now I'll answer your first question. I don't think I have told you about my older brother Quentin who joined the Navy in 1937. He was four years older than I and in 1940 Quentin was home in Mankato on leave. I had previously quit high school to work on a dairy farm for $35.00 a month and my room and board. When it came time to go back to his ship in Bremerton, Washington, Quentin and my Dad came to the dairy farm. Quentin wanted to say goodbye but mostly offer advice and a promise. He told me he wouldn't accept no for an answer and if I went back to finish high school and worked hard he would find a way for the two of us to get a college education when his time was up with the Navy in the summer of 1942. We both promised. It was then that a rather strange thing happened. We weren't much into hugging in those days but Quentin embraced me with a big hug and told me he loved me.

"He went back to his ship and I went back to Loyola High School in Mankato. I made the first string on the football team and sent news clippings about our games to Quentin as we corresponded regularly. I was no longer the class clown in school and earned As and Bs. When I'd send my report card to Quentin, he heaped praise on me and sounded very pleased with me in his letters. In 1941, he wrote that he was concerned about Japan as his battleship was part of the blockade our Navy had to keep Japan from getting much needed war supplies from Indonesia to support their wars against China and Mongolia."

As the bourbon took effect I rambled on with my story. "You may know what's coming, Jim; Pearl Harbor was bombed, Quentin went down with the USS OKLAHOMA and I along with my family was devastated. It was by virtue of my brother's advice that I was later capable of passing the exam for the Army Air Corps cadet program. Over the past nineteen years, Jim, I have often thought of Quentin sitting with his guitar playing and singing 'Life is Like a Mountain Railway.'"

With that Jim got up out of his chair, set his glass on a table, gave me a pat on the back and said, "That's too bad, Giff, I'm sorry to hear that, but it's time we get on with the song." We clicked our glasses after downing their contents and began in harmony.

"Life is like a mountain railway
With an engineer that's brave.
We must make the run successful
From the cradle to the grave.

"Heed the curves and watch the tunnels—
Never falter, never fail.
Keep your hands upon the throttle
And your eye upon the rail.

"Blessed Savior there to guide us
Till we reach that blissful shore,
And the angels there to join us
In God's grace forevermore.

"As you roll across the trestle
Spanning Jordan's swelling tide,
You will reach the Union Depot
Into which your train will ride.

"There you'll meet the superintendent,
God the father, God the son,
With a happy joyous greeting,
'Weary pilgrim, welcome home.'"

As we finished, we thought that we could hear others in song as someone in the joyful celebrating group had the same idea. Jim said, "They probably got the idea from us, Giff. You were really belting it out."

"As a fighter pilot it was part of the program; after a few drinks we'd liven up the party with a night of song." I said. "A strange feeling came over me while we were trying to harmonize. I swear I could feel the presence of my brother Quentin."

Jim said, "Maybe he has been with us all night since taking off from St. Louis. Think about it, maybe he has been assigned as your guardian angel."

"Jim, do you remember if you had a hand on my shoulder when we were looking for the bottom of the clouds?" I asked.

"No, why do you ask?"

"Just think about it." I said. "The party seems to be getting more exciting; do you suppose there's any booze left for a couple of thirsty throttle jockeys?"

"I don't know about you but I need a shower and some shut-eye," Jim said, "so I'm going to say goodnight, Giff—I'll never forget this night together."

"I've corked up for the night and I need some sleep, too. My heartfelt thanks for saving my life," I said. After a vigorous high five we said goodnight and ended our longest day.

* * * * *

## My Older Brother, Quentin

With my older brother Quentin's encouragement, I went back to high school. I went out for football but had no experience coming from a small town at a school that had no sports. The team's center was a senior so I determined to take over his job. Borrowing a football from the coach after football season, I began working my plan. Our team then used the single wing back with the Notre Dame shift. The running back was in motion right or left and the center had to lead him with the ball. To prepare for this, I had my kid sister June swing her tire swing while I practiced snapping the ball through the moving target, moving farther away as I improved. When I became quite proficient at this, I practiced long snapping from great distances.

When practice began in the fall, the coach recognized my talent and I made the team in 1941. Quentin followed my successes with devotion, becoming my mentor and admirer. I sent clippings from our school paper telling of our team's success and my performances, and we sent a Christmas package in which, at his request, I enclosed a framed picture of myself in football gear.

When Pearl Harbor was attacked, there were reports of the USS OKLAHOMA being hit by several torpedoes and capsizing. For the next several days, we lived in hope that Quentin would somehow contact us. On Sunday, December 21, we were having dinner when the phone rang. I answered; it was the Western Union office. We had a telegram from the War Department; the severe snowstorm made it impossible for their messenger to deliver the telegram by bicycle and they asked if we would accept it over the telephone. I handed the phone to my dad, and after listening his legs folded and he slumped to his knees. My dad, who was forty-six at the time, had been stressed for the past two weeks and bordering on depression.

After hearing that Quentin was missing and possibly dead, I picked Dad up and carried him to the couch where he lay holding his hands over his eyes, sobbing. My mother, who was an invalid in a wheel chair, began sobbing when I told her the news. I gave Mom a big hug and kissed her on the cheek, saying, "He's now in heaven, Mom." Seeing my parents who I loved deeply in such misery, I went to my room heartbroken, flopped on my bed and with my face in a pillow, I cried. This is the first time in my young life that I have lost anyone close to me. My younger sisters June, who was four, and Rosemary, age nine, were bewildered over the grief and emotion. Brother Earl, two years older than I, would soon be home from California where he along with many others had gone to get work during the depression. Earl was hoping to join the Navy.

A sense of doom and gloom hung heavily over the Gifford household, from the staggering losses at Pearl Harbor and further advances of the Japanese in the Pacific. President Roosevelt had asked Congress for a declaration of war against Japan and the Axis Powers. It now became obvious that we are in for a long war.

My brother's likely death would hang like an ominous cloud over our household for a long time. It was the end of our lives, as we had known them. My dear mother read the Bible and prayed every day that there had been some mistake and maybe one day he would surprise us and walk in the door. I too had such hopes and dreams about him coming home. Dad just went on about his work and bore his grief in silence but still with a glimmer of hope. My sisters and I continued our school routine and helped around the house, being a comfort to Dad and Mom however we could.

I had inherited the job as cook and housekeeper as my mother's condition worsened. I got up early to make Dad's breakfast and pack a school lunch before getting my sister off to school. At noon, I would jog the one and a half miles home to tend to Mom and make her lunch, and then jog back to school. It was good conditioning for football in the Fall. Life dragged on and Dad spent nights listening to the radio for war news and our greatest joy was sitting around in the living room listening to Whoopi John and his polka band after having Sunday dinner.

On February 9, the other shoe fell like a sledgehammer as the Western Union delivered the message: "The War Department regrets to inform you that your son Quentin John Gifford has been reported as killed in action December 7, 1941."

Quentin's photo appeared in the Mankato Free Press along with his bio. While in boot camp at Great Lakes Naval Training center he had been selected as Honor Man of his company of 96 trainees. He had attained the rank of Petty Officer Second Class and had served with honor as Radioman on the OKLAHOMA.

Soon thereafter the American Legion and the VFW contacted my parents about having a memorial service for Quentin who was one of two servicemen from Mankato to die at Pearl Harbor. It would be held in our large, cathedral-like church, St. Peter and Paul's.

The service was held on a gloomy winter day in mid-February. All of the students from Loyola High attended as well as the grade school students from SS Peter and Paul School, where my sister Rosemary attended. American Legion and VFW members handled the arrangements and provided an Honor Guard. They served as pallbearers with a flag draped catafalque for a casket as there was no body to bury. Relatives and friends from afar attended. It was customary for the Catholic Church to celebrate a High Mass on this occasion. I was an altar boy and got to swing the golden incense boat. As the pungent aromatic grey clouds wafted aloft, I had visions of Quentin in some way being aware of his being honored. I wanted desperately to believe that there exists a form of afterlife with some sort of awareness. It was unimaginable that someone so dearly loved and who loved us so much could be gone from us for all eternity. I guess that's what faith is all about—to assuage that dark and bottomless pit of total despair.

The atmosphere of melancholy from the service was further heightened as the distant soft sound of Taps coming from the choir loft where the Legion bugler so reverently produced the sounds heard by all military for ages.

* * * * *

## My Older Brother, Earl

Brother Earl had returned in time for Quentin's memorial service and soon visited the Navy recruiting office intending to enlist. He had been in a CCC (Civilian Conservation Corps) camp in northern Minnesota and there had been some confusion over his discharge. Because of this, the recruiter would not accept him. It was suggested that he write First Lady Eleanor Roosevelt explaining the situation. We sent the letter and in about a week Earl received a call from the recruiter, saying he had been accepted and should come to be sworn in. On the desk of the recruiter was a letter on White House stationary—a good idea paid off.

Earl became a gunner on a carrier-based torpedo bomber. When the U.S. Marines were re-taking Saipan, his bomber was shot down and crash-landed on the beach as the Marines stormed ashore. The pilot was knocked unconscious and Earl helped pull him out of the wrecked plane. His carrier had been badly damaged and steamed off for Papua New Guinea to a repair base. His crew spent a few days dodging Japanese bullets before being placed on a ship headed for the Island of Eniwetok. From here they boarded a plane destined for the U.S. after pulling a mischievous prank deceiving the transportation personnel about their priority. When in San Francisco, they reported to a Navy office and were sent home to await further orders once the Navy eventually caught up with them. In the meantime, Earl was missing in action as far as they were concerned, and a message to that effect was dispatched to my parents. Fortunately Earl was at home when the message arrived.

## Rod Hundley

"Hot Rod" Hundley will be the first one to admit he's lived a charmed life.

Rod earned All-American honors in 1957 and was the first player taken in the NBA draft by the Minneapolis Lakers. He was the lucky guy at cards that always drew the inside straight, or the upside-down cat that always landed on all fours. Hundley loved to tell about walking away from a plane that had crashed-landed in an Iowa cornfield, and then celebrating his brush with mortality by having a snowball fight with his fellow passengers.

Rod played for six seasons with the Lakers, broadcast for New Orleans for five years and 35 years for Utah Jazz, being inducted into the Broadcasters Hall of Fame.

"The things that have happened to me have been wonderful," Hundley says.

# Carroll Daily Times Herald

Vol. 91—No. 14    Return Postage Guaranteed    Carroll, Iowa, Monday, January 18, 1960—Eight Pages    Delivered by Carrier Boy Each Evening for 35 Cents Per Week. 7¢ Single Copy

# 23 Safe as Passenger Plane Lands in Carroll Corn Field in Snow Storm

**New Storm Dumps 5 In. Snow Here**

About 15 In. Now; Battle to Keep Highways Open

Another blustery snowstorm swept over Carroll County Monday night and Tuesday morning, piling an estimated five additional inches on top of the nine and one-half inches that fell in last week's blizzard. That left the area blanketed by nearly 15 inches of snow.

Temperatures continued cold as city, county and state snowplow crews battled drifting snow. There was a five degree drop from 13 degrees at 7 a.m. to 13 at 10 a.m. Sunday's readings ranged from a low of 8 to a high of 13. State highway commission crews went out at 1 a.m. Monday and will remain out as long as needed. Right pieces of equipment were in operation on the main roads.

**Minneapolis Pro Cage Team Aboard**

Pilot Brings Big Craft Down in 'Magnificent Landing' Without Radio or Defroster; Visibility Zero

A twin-engined passenger plane carrying 10 members of the Minneapolis Lakers professional basketball team and 13 other persons made an emergency landing in a corn field about a half mile north of 18th street and east of Grant Road at 1:40 a.m. Monday.

The huge DC-3 transport, owned by the Lakers, and serviced by Gopher Aviation Company, Wold-Chamberlain field, Minneapolis, landed without damage in a heavy snow storm and without radio, defroster or lights in zero visibility.

**Icing, Engine Missing**

Vernon Ullman, Brookings, S.D., a retired Marine Air Force pilot with the rank of lieutenant colonel, set the plane down here because he had been forced down from an altitude of 17,000 feet by icing conditions and a missing engine.

"We left St. Louis about 8:30 p.m. Sunday and had to co-pilot said. "About five minutes after take-off we lost everything electrical. Both generators cut out and we had no radio or heat. We climbed to 3,000 feet and were in the clear for about 15 minutes. Then the storm closed in and we lost our visual contacts."

**'Miracle Landing'—**

A 'miracle' landing in over one foot of snow in a field of standing, unpicked corn, was made here early Monday morning by Vernon Ullman, pilot of a twin-engined transport bearing the Minneapolis Lakers professional basketball team on a trip from St. Louis, Mo., to Minneapolis, Minn. The pilot set the plane down in the corn field on the Mrs. Henna Steffes farm north of Carroll. The plane rolled to a stop at a point four-tenths of a mile north of 18th street and a couple hundred yards east of Grant Road. The landing was made at 1:40 a.m. in a blinding snow storm after the plane

had circled over Carroll for nearly three-quarters of an hour. Mr. Ullman said all electrical equipment on the plane failed about five minutes after take-off at St. Louis about 1:20 p.m. and it was impossible to return to the St. Louis airport or to find another airport without radio contact. He had been flying at an altitude of 17,000 feet, of course, and had to come down when one engine started missing and the air speed dropped to 50 knots, about 90 miles per hour. (Staff Photo) (MORE PICTURES, Page 8.)

# 11

# THE BUS RIDE HOME

Iknew the effects of adrenalin from past experience and how it could affect the body after an extended period of great anxiety, and I was wide-awake. After finishing the cigar and last drops of bourbon, I decided a hot shower would further warm my tired and chilled bones.

It was past three in the morning when I finally attempted to get some rest. At first sleep didn't come easy as my mind wandered over the past several hours. The next thing I was aware of was a knock on my door and Jim saying, "They have a bus lined up for a ride to Minneapolis and I think some ladies from the Elks Club are serving breakfast for all of us." Looking at my watch it read 7:15 and I had gotten some sleep after all. That bourbon really did the trick.

After dressing, I joined the others for breakfast as Jim and I found an empty table. While we had a great breakfast with coffee, pancakes and eggs with sausage, we noticed the reporters flocking around Verne for their stories. Jim said, "I bet he hopes they don't talk to us," and they didn't just then.

Someone had begun circulating placemats, which we all signed as memorabilia. It was announced that we would be going home by bus in a few hours. Many graceful townspeople came to wish us well as they offered to help us in any way that they could. We would soon be departing from a place that will forever be remembered with deep appreciation and fondness.

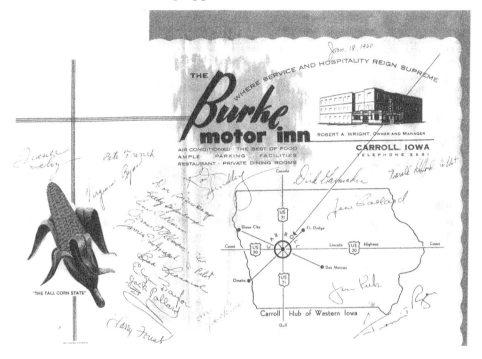

On the trip home some were sleeping after a night of celebrating as others were joyfully chatting about their adventure. Elgin was trying to find a deck of cards so he could make a few bucks off his teammates. As we passed the cornfield where we saw our airplane, someone exclaimed, "Look at that big deep ditch just a short distance ahead of the airplane. We could have been killed had we flipped over there." Jim and I looked at each other and laughed as we noticed the dark cloud shadow just beyond the airplane. That field was perfectly flat for at least a quarter of a mile. I guess that's how rumors get started.

I felt a renewed interest in life and how fortunate I was to be alive and flying for a living. While pondering the many additional adventures awaiting me, I was excited about being a pilot with the Air Force Reserve. I owed a lot to the Air Force for all the intensive training and experience that I have been privileged to have. All of the link trainer time going back to 1943 and the more modern flight simulator training had paid off big time.

I figured that should I continue to have the same number of safe landings as takeoffs I would have another twelve years of Air Force Reserve flying. In commercial and corporate aviation I should have over thirty years of adventure awaiting me. By the time I retired, I could have a lot of stories to tell.

A very progressive aviation company, Gopher Aviation, was my employer. Gopher Aviation was a very active Beechcraft distributor having the latest models of their entire line in their inventory. Gopher was the largest overhaul facility for radial engines. I had many adventuresome duties such as air taxi, contract pilot service for corporations, and demonstration of new aircraft. I had test-flown aircraft that had been repaired or modified. The dawn of the golden years in private and commercial aviation was about to break for me.

All of northern Iowa and southern Minnesota had been clobbered with snow from the storm. The wind was still causing the snow to drift and swirl making driving slow and hazardous. The windows on our bus were frosted from the extreme cold making the bleak countryside look somewhat surreal. I could hardly wait to get back home and bring this nightmare to a close. Though I had been without much sleep, I was weary but not very sleepy.

Jim had been trying to catch a few winks but with little success. He turned toward me and said, "Giff, has it occurred to you that if we hadn't lost electrical power we might not have made it?"

"Why do you say that?"

"Well, look at it this way. We know the sky was loaded with heavy icing in the front and we had filed our flight plan for eight thousand feet hard altitude and that's where the bad stuff was. Had we flown into a patch of heavy icing we could have really been goners. Icing can come on fast and furious. That's why it's in FAA Regulations not to file into an area of known heavy icing."

"That's what happened to the famous movie producer, Mike Todd, who married Liz Taylor," I told Jim. "In 1958, while on a flight from Los Angeles to New York in his own Lockheed Lodestar, they encountered heavy icing over the Zuni Mountains at two in the morning and called Flight Service requesting a different altitude to get out of the ice. That was their last radio transmission. When encountering heavy icing with minimum de-icing capability it happens quickly and then it's too late. The wreckage was scattered over half a mile area on a mountain plateau.

"Remember Clark Gable's wife, Carol Lombard, back in 1942? She, along with twenty-one others, flying on a TWA DC-3 Sky Sleeper crashed into a mountain in Nevada shortly after departing Las Vegas for L.A. They were flying the beam at night when they disappeared. Icing may have been the problem but not too likely. That airplane was the same as the one we almost crashed last night and the flight panel and instruments were about the same as ours.

"The bird I've been flying in the Air Force has the best anti-icing system. The C-119 Boxcar has eight 250,000 BTU gasoline heaters installed above the cargo compartment between the wings. Heat is ducted to the leading edge of wing and tail flying surfaces and to the engine accessory section for engine pre-heating. Heat is also provided for the cockpit and cargo compartment.

"It seems ironic but our situation enabled us to use our experience and knowledge of weather to do our thing and avoid the heavy icing. You might say there was some luck and perhaps Providential guidance involved in finding that cornfield. If we hadn't found it I'm not so sure what we could have done."

"In a way I hate to think of all the second-guessing we'll hear from the brotherhood of fellow pilots." Jim said. "They'll be trying to figure out where we screwed up; most aircraft accidents and incidents are considered pilot error."

"What accident are you talking about?" I said. "There was no accident. Accidents are when the airplane is bent or someone is injured or killed. That's the reason I was for landing with the gear extended. Had we landed with gear up we'd have been required to file an accident report with a thorough investigation by the Feds. All we had was a deviation from our flight plan and an unscheduled landing—though they may try to hang us for failing to close our flight plan with Flight Service," I replied with a chuckle.

"You know, we've never had much time to shoot the breeze and I've been wanting to ask you about your past flying experience," Jim said. "How'd you get started in flying after the war?"

"After the war—that was over fourteen years ago—I was on a troop ship passing under the Golden Gate Bridge on a chilly foggy April morning in 1946. I thought I'd freeze to death in

Frisco after being on tropical Guam where the temperature hovers around 91 degrees year round. I was sent to Fort Lewis in Tacoma, Washington for separation and then by train to Billings, Montana where my wife and baby daughter were with her sister and family. It was great to see them; my daughter, Gaylyn, was about eight months old.

"The next day I took my military flight record to the Billings CAA office [ed. note: this was the Civil Aeronautics Administration which was the predecessor of the FAA] and I was given a test after which I received a commercial pilot license. While hanging around the Billings airport a few days, I finally found a pilot who was looking to hire a flight instructor. He was going to establish a training program in Choteau, Montana for pilots taking advantage of the G.I. Bill. Well, I was not a flight instructor but that wasn't a problem—I'd become one. I liked the idea of living in Montana, the 'Big Country,' so we agreed on a deal and I would be there after Easter.

"Jim, you are probably getting tired of listening to me but when I start talking flying I don't know when to stop." Our bus pulled into a truck stop for gas and lunch. "Sometime when we have a flight together I'll finish the story."

\* \* \* \* \*

## Bob Short, Minneapolis Lakers Owner

Robert Earl Short (July 20, 1917-November 20, 1982) was an American businessman, sports teams owner and politician.

Short graduated from the College of Saint Thomas (now the University of St. Thomas) in St. Paul, Minnesota before receiving his law degree from Georgetown University Law Center. He enlisted in the United States Navy during World War II, rising from Ensign in 1942 to commander before he resigned in 1946. He married the former Marion D. McCann in 1948 and they settled in Edina, Minnesota, where they raised 7 children.

Short practiced law for several years and started to invest in business ventures after buying an interest in a small trucking line, Mueller Transportation. He built the company into a major freight carrier known as Admiral Merchants Motor Freight. He later expanded into real estate and the hotel business. From these investments he later purchased two professional sports teams.

Short was a long-time supporter of the University of Notre Dame and served as a member of the school's Law School Advisory Council from 1974 until his death in 1982, when he was succeeded by his wife in both business and at Notre Dame (she also served nine years on the board of trustees of what became the University of Saint Thomas). He endowed the Robert and Marion Short Chair in Law at the Notre Dame Law School, where his son attended.

Short bought the cellar-dwelling Minneapolis Lakers of the National Basketball Association in the late 1950s and moved the team to Los Angeles in 1960 due to terrible attendance in the-then small Twin Cities market, where hockey was favored and iconic George Mikan had retired in the early 50s. The Lakers immediately resumed their winning ways in L.A., resulting from increased attendance and revenue. Short sold the team in 1974.

\* \* \* \* \*

## Flying with the Short Family

After moving the team to Los Angeles, Bob Short sold the famous DC-3 and purchased a twin Beech airplane for personal and business trips. I had many fun trips in this airplane, flying Mr. Short and some of his staff and politicians. I had flown on campaign trips with Hubert Humphrey, Governor Mondale and Ted Kennedy.

During a presidential campaign season, I had flown Mr. Short and Senator Hubert Humphrey to a small town in South Dakota where the runway was a grass strip in the middle of a cornfield. When we were about to depart, the Senator had asked if he could ride in the co-pilot seat and I had responded with, "Be my guest, Senator." As the Senator looked ahead through the windscreen he remarked that the runway didn't appear to be long enough. I had pointed to a spot about one thousand feet ahead at the intersection with another runway and said, "We'll be in the air by that spot," as the Senator gave me a doubtful look. I moved to the extreme end of the runway, checked the magnetos, lowered fifteen degrees of flaps and ran up the engines before releasing the brakes. As we rolled into the wind I was able to lift off shortly before the spot that I had indicated. After retracting the gear and flaps I noticed the Senator just shaking his head as he said, "I don't know how you do it."

On one particular trip I flew the entire Short family from Florida to Minnesota. Brian, who was about eleven years old at the time, sat in the co-pilot seat for the entire trip. Based on all the questions Brian asked about what's this for and what does that do and how do I learn to fly, I thought that he would some day be an airline or military pilot.

Throughout the next fifty years I was known as the guy in the right seat of an airplane that had landed in an Iowa cornfield with the Lakers onboard, and I was often asked to tell the story.

### Frank Selvy[1]

Frank is best remembered for scoring 100 points in a college game for South Carolina's Furman University against Newberry College in 1954, the only NCAA Division 1 player to do so. The game was played near the end of Selvy's college career and the coach had designated that game as "Frank Selvy Night" to garner recognition for the player who was certain to finish the season leading the nation in scoring and to earn first-team All-American honors—both of these accomplishments he had already earned the previous year. The game was the first to be broadcast live on television. Many from his hometown, including his family, had made the six-hour trip.

The coach had simply suggested the team get the ball to Selvy so he could score as much as possible, and he did so—making 41 of 66 baskets and 18 of 22 free throws. His last score came from a desperate shot from mid-court at the buzzer. This game was played long before the three-point rule and it was estimated that at least a dozen of his shots would have counted as three points today.

Selvy was chosen first overall by the Baltimore Bullets in the 1954 NBA draft, and he went on to play nine seasons in the NBA during the late fifties and early sixties, interrupted by a three-year hitch in the US Army.

Selvy is most famous for his time with the Lakers, teaming with Jerry West, Hundley and Elgin Baylor, twice becoming an NBA All

---

1    Source: Steve Ashburner, NBA.com, used with permission

Star.

The Lakers faced the Celtics in the 1962 finals and had a 3 to 2 game lead before returning to L.A. for game six. Selvy recalled, of game six, "I was five for five from the field guarding Sam Jones and he hadn't scored a point. We had a 17-point lead. Then I get put on the bench, and by the time I come back in we're down by 10. Maybe Hot Rod can explain *that*."

This was Selvy's response to Rod Hundley's ribbing about his missed shot in game seven, when the Lakers were down by four points with seconds left on the clock and Selvy had grabbed two rebounds and scored four points to tie the game. With five seconds on the clock, Selvy inbounded the pass to Hundley at mid-court, who dribbled to the top of the key, pump-faked a pass to West who was covered and then spotted Selvy in the left corner. Hundley said he could have taken a shot and if he made it he could be Mayor of L.A. but if he missed he'd be run out of town. Seeing Selvy open for an 18-foot shot he fed the ball to him and perhaps his arm was bumped by Cousy causing the shot to miss putting the game in overtime. Had Selvy scored that shot the Lakers would have won the Championship, which they then failed to do until 1985.

Selvy, who played six of his nine NBA seasons with the Lakers, also knows that no one shot makes or breaks an entire series. He thinks the Lakers should have won the championship in game six, when they took an early lead before Boston roared back in the third quarter and blew them out, 119-105. He's still mystified as to why he spent much of that game on the bench, watching Hundley play in his place.

Not long after that loss in game seven, Selvy began receiving telephone calls with a muffled voice proclaiming "Nice shot" followed by a hang-up. This happened many times throughout the next several years. When being needled by Hundley, Selvy would come back with, "If I'd have been in there in game six instead of you we could have won the Championship."

Baylor said he has thought about the "what if"—if the Lakers had won that series, would it have had a wider effect on more than a decade of Boston dominance. The Celtics won 11 titles between 1957 and 1969.

"It could possibly have changed things," Baylor said. "We always thought that we could win. We never thought we were going to lose. We just felt that we were good enough to win."

# 12

# "HOME WAS NEVER SO GOOD"

### *January 18, 1960*

We stopped in Clear Lake, Iowa, near Mason City where Buddy Holly, Ritchie Valens and the Big Bopper had tragically bought the farm only eleven months earlier. That had been February 3, 1959, now known as "the day the music died".

Everyone went to grab a bite while the driver gassed up the bus. A quick glance at the menu and I knew just what I wanted. These Iowa truck stops were famous for their hot roast beef sandwiches with mashed potatoes and gravy so that's what I ordered, and Jim had the same plus a slice of warm freshly baked apple pie with ice cream. The cooks in these places were usually ladies from a local church who often cooked for large gatherings like funerals and weddings—and they knew how to cook.

We all piled in the warm bus for the rest of the trip home. The driver said it would take another four to five hours due to the snow-packed roads and blowing snow. Jim and I slouched down in our seats and I became drowsy after the big meal and the cozy warm bus. We were about to finally doze off when Coach Jim Pollard approached us and said, "You two guys really deserve a lot of credit for saving all of our lives. I was right behind you looking over your shoulders and what I witnessed was an amazing display of calm, skill and talent being applied to get us safely on the ground. I'll never forget the experience and I'll always be grateful to you two—so will all the other passengers."

"Thanks, Jim; the only time I was really shaken up was when we nearly slammed it into those trees. I'm thankful for your support and lobbying for the cornfield, which finally convinced Verne to listen." Frank Ryan and several team members came to Jim and I sitting in the back and expressed their appreciation for saving their lives by finding and landing in the cornfield.

As we were on our way again things quieted down and nearly all passengers were dozing. Jim and I had been over thirty hours without very much sleep and now with our stomachs full and the warmth of the bus we both dropped off into a badly needed deep sleep.

When I finally awakened, it was nearly dark and we were not far from the airport and the FBO where the passengers had parked their cars. I imagine that if we hadn't made it, saddened family members would be retrieving their cars and making funeral arrangements though it would be unlikely that the burned wreckage would have yielded much of our remains.

We pulled into the parking lot and unloaded, and after grabbing luggage and saying brief farewells the passengers were off to their cars and home. Jim and I had parked our cars over at Fleming Field in South St. Paul, so we bummed a ride from a De Ponti Aviation employee to Fleming Field.

The thirty-minute drive to my home in Richfield passed quickly and I soon pulled into my driveway. After turning off the ignition, I sat there and thought about the past twenty-some hours from when we took off from St. Louis to when I finally turned off the magneto switches after we landed. There was a moment when we flew north from Carroll that I considered that we might not make it and I might not be home now.

There were many hugs and kisses from my wife and kids, 14-year-old Gaylyn, 12-year-old Doug and John, who was 8. I slouched into an overstuffed chair as John pulled off my shoes and propped my feet up. My wife, Alvina, said, "How about if I fix a hot toddy for you, Giff?"

"That sounds great, but go easy on the booze and heavy on the honey and lemon—and make it extra hot, I still feel a chill from that long, cold flight," I replied. The adrenalin had worn off and I was beginning to relax. The hot toddy sent a very warm feeling flooding through my veins. Home was never so good.

They were all talking at the same time, as they were anxious to hear about what had happened to me. "Were you scared? Did anyone get hurt? How bad is the airplane?" were the questions.

"Someone called earlier saying that the airplane was missing," my wife said, and had asked if she'd heard from me. After receiving that call there was a lot of fear and some crying from the thought that I might have been killed. Doug later told me that they had prayed for my safety.

"Now are you going to tell us all about it?" my wife said, the kids chiming in with questions.

By now the hot toddy had warmed me through and loosened my tongue. "Less than 24 hours ago we had an emergency power failure after leaving St. Louis. Five and a half hours later we all nearly died in a terrible snowstorm. Fortunately we made it and I'm here with you all safe and sound—and I think I smell roast beef." In a moment I had a tray on my lap with a plate heaped with mashed potatoes, and a hot beef sandwich smothered in gravy. After the hot toddy and food I became very sleepy. I explained to my family that I had practically no sleep since Saturday night and asked to be excused until tomorrow.

Lying comfortably in my own bed, I momentarily reflected on how things would be in this house for my family had I not made it. Before falling into a sound sleep I mentally uttered a prayer of thanks for the help in providing me with what it took to survive.

# 13

# VISITS FROM FRIENDS

What a difference a good night's sleep makes. I awoke to the smell of freshly brewed coffee and a quiet house as the kids were off to school and the wife was at her bowling day with the Officers' wives club. I found the pot of coffee and some fresh donuts when the phone rang. My boss at Gopher Aviation was the first to call; since he had already gotten the scoop from Verne, there wasn't much to tell. He told me to take the day off and he'd see me tomorrow. Many family members called and were happy to hear my voice. Fellow pilots from the Air Force called to hear the story.

Carl Taylor, one of the other DC-3 captains, called and asked if he could stop by and I said, "Come on over, I've got the coffee pot on." Carl was usually very quiet and when he spoke he chose his words carefully. On layovers when we flew the Lakers, Carl and I would take long walks around the town with hardly a word spoken. Having flown the DC-3 in Central and South America for many years without a co-pilot, Carl was unique in our profession and usually had his own way of doing things.

The doorbell rang and after letting Carl in, he shook my hand and said, "It's good to see you. I was worried when I heard you were overdue and hadn't been heard from." After settling down with a cup of hot coffee Carl glanced over his cup, looking me straight in the eye as he sipped without saying a word. He set his cup on the coffee table and asked in a quiet and serious voice, "What went wrong?"

I covered the events as I had remembered, and Carl asked, "Is it OK if I light my pipe?"

"No problem."

Carl sat, drawing on his pipe and said, "You guys did well with the mess you were in; however, it would have helped if you had a fully charged battery before leaving."

"I remember we were unable to start an engine on the battery power and I suggested that we have a quick charge but Verne had said that the generators would charge the battery."

"That could have had a lot to do with the generator failure because the generators were overburdened by recharging the battery," Carl offered. "Landing in that field really saved your butts. You would have run out of fuel before finding better weather."

"Do you know what's on the team's schedule?" I asked.

"I think you and I are flying the team to the west coast next week, if they get the plane back here in working order," he replied. The phone rang as Carl rose to leave, saying we could talk about it on our trip next week. It was the FAA calling; they wanted to see me in their office at the terminal at 1 PM.

My old friend, Bill Berg, called next. He was a North Central Airline captain flying the DC-3 and a fellow C-119 pilot in the AF Reserve. Bill was in the area and asked if he could visit for a little while.

Bill was always wearing a big smile and made me feel that he really enjoyed my company. We flew together in formation in the F-80 jets and the C-119 Boxcar and we flew the Mustang; we had a lot of fun on long trips. We had the time of our lives on a trip to Bermuda when we stayed at the Elbow Beach Surf Club in April, the peak of the tourist season. It was then that I bought the tailor-made heavy wool Harris Tweed suit that I wore on the trip to St. Louis.

After many years as captain on the DC-3 with North Central, I found Bill to be a very good teacher. I learned a lot about avoiding ice, penetration of thunderstorms and low visibility approaches. These guys were as close as they could get to flying by the seat of their pants. With limited navigation, communication equipment and air navigation facilities, flying from the Dakotas to Detroit and many points between was a challenge. These guys spent most of the time at altitudes where the weather was the worst. In battling thunderstorms, icing, snow and fog, they had to employ great skill, cunning and often daring tactics in order to do their job successfully.

The doorbell rang and Bill greeted me with a big smile and a slap on the shoulder. "Giffy, old buddy, what the hell happened? We damn near lost you. You guys are all over the news—that's one heck of a way to gain attention. I'd guess that you had a lot to do with handling the problem after all I taught you."

"Thanks, Bill, I guess I owe you a couple beers."

"I'm glad you made it, because I'm about to leave for a two-week vacation and I'd have hated to miss the funeral," Bill said with a chuckle.

I put on another pot of coffee and Bill said, "I'll take mine black, and I could use one of those donuts, too." We sat in the living room with the fireplace shedding its warmth and the flames creating an ambience conducive to comfort and good conversation.

It took me only about fifteen minutes to give Bill an outline of the time leading up to the flight and the landing. Bill listened with his customary pensive manner and after a long sip of coffee he looked at me and said, "Did you say that you tried a battery start and the battery wouldn't handle it?"

"Yes, and you are about to tell me I should have refused to go with a nearly dead battery."

"No, my friend, you were in a sort of predicament. Having a wife and three kids to feed, a job was pretty important. I'd say that your leader should explain why he didn't give instructions on how to contact him when he left with his wife and passengers. Had you been able to contact him with your concerns about the weather and heavy icing en route, that might have prevented having everyone in position ready to go. Backing out of the flight would have been rather awkward for Verne. This is a dangerous situation and usually leads to irrational decisions."

"Not only did we have twenty passengers anxious to get home but also a company that we felt responsible to for keeping expenses down," I said.

"You know, Giff, this is a classic example of 'get home-itis;' it causes many airplane disasters. If you had refused to go, Verne may have gone without you using the student co-pilot. Had the flight been completed with no problem, you could have had trouble.

From what I'm hearing, if the power failure had occurred without you in the right seat, it likely would have ended in disaster."

"The truth is, Bill, had we crashed it would have been my error. I should have realized that something was not quite right with Verne. When I lost the road and asked if he had it, I should have been more specific. Had I known he didn't have the road I would have made the missed approach that I eventually had to do to avoid certain death."

"You were under stress and anxiety for over five hours and running on adrenalin; you couldn't expect to be perfect. If it were not for the alertness on Jim's part and your quick response, you'd have had it," said Bill.

"Yeah, that's as close to death as anyone would care to be," I said.

The phone rang and Bill left, saying he'd check in later. Our Air Force Reserve Group commanding officer was on the line telling me he was happy that I made it and he looked forward to seeing me on the training weekend and hearing all about it. After chatting a few minutes, I realized that I had an appointment with the FAA.

I parked in the airport terminal lot and went to their office. I was asked to show my pilot's certificate and annual physical record, and then the questions began. I stayed pretty much with the storyline as reported to the media by Verne and avoided making any waves and further questioning. The only criticism they had was we didn't close out our instrument flight plan until the next morning. After what we'd been through that wasn't high on my priority list.

\* \* \* \* \*

## Carl Taylor, Another Lakers' Pilot

Carl is one of the pilots that I had the pleasure of flying with on many DC-3 trips. We also had many flights together in the jet Commander and twin Beech.

Carl had gained notoriety later in his career when he repossessed a jet from Idi Amin, the brutal dictator of Uganda. Idi Amin had purchased a jet from Israeli Aircraft but had not paid for the purchase. Several attempts to collect were futile. Carl, having been highly qualified in that type of aircraft, had been solicited to train an aircrew for Idi Amin. Carl worked a deal with the aircraft company to repossess the jet. During the training, Carl had reported a mechanical problem with the brakes or engine reversing system and said that he had to perform a high-speed taxi test on the runway. He had convinced the Ugandans that this required minimum crew only. The high-speed test became a takeoff and Carl headed for Tel Aviv, where he returned the jet. I assume that Carl had received a substantial bonus for performing such a risky task.

I had met with Carl only occasionally over the next few years until I saw him early one morning when I was about to depart on a charter trip from Burlington Northern Aeromotive. Carl had a very early start from La Crosse, Wisconsin, and sometime around midnight that same day Carl had the misfortune of crashing while attempting to land an MU-2 in Michigan in bad weather. It was a very sad funeral for my old friend.

\* \* \* \* \*

## An Analysis of My Mistakes

As pilots, we religiously read the reports of aircraft accidents and look especially for the probable cause. Had we crashed and all had perished I have no idea what the NTSB would have listed as the probable cause. Looking back to that night I now realize that I had fumbled the ball four times but fortunately I had recovered them.

The first fumble was when I did not refuse to be a part of initiating a flight into known heavy icing. The second fumble was when I failed to mutiny and demand landing in the cornfield after having found it. The third was when I foolishly turned the controls over to Verne when I lost the road; he couldn't possibly have had the road when he hadn't been looking out his window. The fourth and possibly the most crucial one was when upon losing the road I should have executed the missed approach that I soon did to avoid the trees. We may have made it, but had I not committed those fumbles we would not have come so close to dying.

# 14

# BACK TO THE
# AIR TAXI BOOTH

Life slowly returned to normal as Jim and I manned our air
taxi booth at the old terminal. A local TV station called and
asked if we could fly a reporter to Winona where the jury was
deliberating after a famous murder trial. The weather was not too
good with low ceilings and haze but Winona was expected to improve soon. North Central Airlines couldn't promise them they'd
get into the airport and asked if we cared to give it a try. A check
with aviation weather revealed low ceilings but surface visibility
was variable from two to five miles. I was very familiar with the
Mississippi River and the location of Winona near an island and
a large bend in the river. I called the TV station and arranged a
pickup location and time for their reporter.

Soon we were loaded in the Bonanza and ready to taxi. I requested a special VFR clearance out of the area and proceeded
with the scud running flight down the Mississippi. My main concern was the various lines strung across the river but they were
easily detected with warning banners hanging from most of them.
I recognized the towns of Hastings, Red Wing and Wabasha and
soon I saw an island in the distance that is near Winona. I contacted Winona with information of my position and intentions. I

landed, dropped off my passenger with his equipment and headed to a nearby grill for lunch.

Fortunately, the jury reached a verdict by mid-afternoon and my passenger's job was done so we were ready to go before dark. We flew back up the Mississippi as daylight began to fade. Over Hastings, I contacted Minneapolis approach control and requested special VFR into the area and vectors to runway 11 R. After leaving my passenger at the FBO, I taxied to the hangar where we kept the Bonanza.

Back in our air taxi booth I found a note that Carl and I were scheduled for a west coast trip with the Lakers next Tuesday, January 26.

I later learned that our first destination was Seattle, where Elgin Baylor had attended the University of Washington. What would have been a home game with Cincinnati with less than one thousand in attendance would be played in Seattle to a sellout crowd.

Later in the week, Jim and I were on standby in the air taxi booth waiting for business and reading the morning Minneapolis Tribune when we saw the front page of the Sports section—we were shocked. A large photo showed Verne receiving an award for his skillful performance by saving the team on the flight from St. Louis. A special event was held in his honor during which Verne had been presented a plaque from Mr. Short and a trophy for which the team members and others had each donated fifty dollars in appreciation. After reading the entire story, Jim and I looked at each other and shook our heads. Jim said, "I wonder why we weren't invited to the party. Did anyone call you, Giff?"

"No, not a word from anyone. I just don't get it. Did the high altitude on the flight affect his memory and he can't recall what really happened?"

"Heck, no," Jim said. "He knows what happened and just didn't want us there to tell our version of what went on."

Just then, Verne showed up at the booth and immediately saw the newspaper story. "Didn't they call you guys?" Verne asked, pointing at the paper. "I thought that you guys just didn't show up." Jim and I were speechless as we stood there looking at each other in disbelief. Verne took out his wallet and offered a couple twenties to Jim and I but we refused to take anything. We both left Verne in the booth and went to the airport café on the upper level for a cup of coffee.

Jim and I puzzled over Verne's behavior and decided there was nothing to do but put it behind us. We learned a lesson in human behavior—things don't always turn out the way they should. In business, and especially the flying business, it was best to leave things as they were and move on. The story as it was reported was OK with the company; the real story could have negative results for our employer.

Meanwhile the basketball team met with owner Bob Short telling him that they had voted in a democratic manner against flying on the company airplane. Mr. Short replied that he was the leader of the democracy and if they wanted a job they would be on the next flight.

The next four games had been scheduled as home games against Cincinnati, Syracuse and Philadelphia. Arrangements were made to fly these teams to the west coast at the Lakers' expense. Advance PR had arranged for stadiums and they were sold out in a short time at premium rates. This represented a huge profit; the four home games would have sold between four and five thousand tickets total compared to more than twice that for each game in Seattle, Portland, Oakland, and Los Angeles. The Seattle game was scheduled for January 27.

Fleming Field, the South St. Paul airport, was just coming alive with mechanics and others coming to work as Carl and I had our trusty old bird pulled out of the hangar. With a full load of fuel, a complete walk-around inspection, and all needed supplies for the passengers, we took off for the Minneapolis airport where we parked at De Ponti Aviation to pick up our passengers. We allowed ourselves an hour and a half to check on the weather and stock the ice cooler, coffee container and other supplies.

I filed a VFR (Visual Flight Rules) flight plan to Rapid City, South Dakota, our first rest and re-fuel stop. We would then fly to Missoula, Montana for another pit stop, and then on to Seattle.

The trip west was uneventful except for one thing. Carl was not too hot about filing a flight plan unless it was definitely IFR (Instrument Flight Rules) weather. Without his knowledge, I would file a VFR flight plan which required reporting to Flight Service information such as departure point, route of flight, destination and time en-route. If it became necessary to file an IFR flight plan, it was just a matter of calling Flight Service and requesting an IFR. As we neared the mountains, we were in and out of cloud tops and when I suggested filing an IFR, Carl kept putting it off until we were solid IFR. I put in the call and we were given a hard altitude and a route clearance to Missoula. The next leg to Seattle went well; it was raining there but not very cold.

The Lakers won the game and Elgin scored thirty-six points. The next leg to Portland was a short hop and the team lost to Syracuse before a packed house. The next day we flew to Oakland where the team lost to Philadelphia. We got an earlier start the following day and flew down the coastline to Los Angeles, where they were to play Philadelphia again.

A funny thing happened in Los Angeles. While I was watching the game on TV in our hotel lobby, I was approached by a man who noticed my interest in the Lakers. He asked if I was with the team and I told him that I was one of their pilots. He said that he was a personnel manager with the L.A. Dodgers who had recently moved to L.A. and had heard about our cornfield landing. He told me that he was hiring pilots to fly their airplane and asked if I was interested. I became suspicious when he asked me to his room to fill out an application. I declined and excused myself, heading to my room to watch the game.

In L.A. it was raining and rather cool. When we cranked up the engines for our return trip, there was an occasional backfire due to the moisture in the magnetos. As I glanced back into the cabin I sensed some concern as all eyes were focused on the cockpit. Carl told me to assure them that it was normal after the bird had been sitting in the rain. During the climb out over Disneyland, there was still an occasional backfire. I turned toward the cabin and gave the passengers the thumbs up meaning not to worry, but by the looks on their faces I wasn't sure if they were buying my assurance.

The remainder of the trip was uneventful and we soon settled back into the same old routine.

I flew on several more trips to the east coast and in between. Whenever we landed, the control tower operator would remark about seeing our airplane on the headlines of their paper.

When the team eventually moved to L.A., an era of special adventure for me had come to an end. I really enjoyed being around those great guys.

Verne eventually left Gopher Aviation. The pilots at Southern Airways were out on strike and aircrews were being hired as replacements. Verne applied but he was unable to demonstrate his ability to fly as an air transport pilot on the DC-3. Jim was hired as a co-pilot and flew with the airline until the strike ended.

# 15

# THE REUNION

In 2009 I received a phone call from John Steffes in Carroll. John was happy to find me still alive after all this time and he explained his plans for a reunion on January 18, 2010 and invited Jim Holznagel and I. John was an experienced promoter and soon the plans for the event were complete. By the end of 2009, the event was gaining the attention of the Sports Media.

### *January 18, 2010*

On this Sunday morning cars from Woodbury, Mora, Willmar, and Annandale, Minnesota departed for Carroll, Iowa. Another car had departed Tallahassee, Florida on the seventeenth. After an overnight in St. Louis, my son, Doug, and his wife, Sandra, had headed for Carroll as they drove over the approximate route that we had flown over in 1960. My stepson, John, and his wife, Lou Anne, drove for my wife, Carol and I. Jim Holznagel and his wife drove from Mora. My brother, Earl, and his wife, June, departed Willmar with Bob Schuman, my brother in law, and his wife, Donna. We were all headed for Carroll to celebrate an event that nearly terminated my life at age thirty-six. Considering the fifty years that I have enjoyed living since then, this anniversary was a big deal for me.

Driving was hampered by fog and very low visibility but

when we arrived at the hotel in Carroll we received a very warm welcome from John Steffes, Mayor Pedelty and Airport Director Norm Hutcheson. Soon all the others arrived and it was almost like a family reunion.

I had made arrangements with Don Menson, Carroll Airport Manager, to charter an airplane and sort of re-enact the flight from when we had spotted the water tower at Carroll, but we had to scrub the flight due to very bad fog. Our gang all met in the Hotel Café for a late lunch with discussion about that night half a century ago. Later we rested for a bit in our rooms before the evening event.

When we arrived at the Chamber of Commerce meeting hall, the place was packed with locals and media. There was a huge fiftieth anniversary cake that Jim and I were privileged to cut as photographers zoomed in on us. There were a lot of introductions with questions about the flight and picture-taking with the many local dignitaries and residents.

After being introduced, Jim told the compelling story about his experience of riding in the jump seat behind Verne and I on that scary night. He talked of finding enough flashlights to last until we landed; how he backed up the pilots in watching our flight instruments, especially our airspeed and altitude; how he was the liaison between Verne, myself, and the passengers. All those present listened very attentively, in silence. In spite of reliving what had happened fifty years ago, the people of Carroll were happy to hear our side of the story. All they knew was that a large airplane circling their city in a snowstorm at one in the morning without any lights had to be in serious trouble. Jim finished his story and was given a standing ovation. All present realized the importance of his contribution to saving the lives of all on board.

As John Steffes introduced me, I felt proud and honored. I began by voicing my opinion about being called a hero. "According to Webster's dictionary," I said, "a hero is a mythological or legendary figure, often of divine descent, endowed with great strength or ability or an illustrious warrior. In modern day thinking a hero is one who risks his own life to save the life of others. Neither Jim nor I fit that definition. The truth is, we were primarily concerned with saving our own lives. The passengers, while enduring the agony and fear of a disastrous crash, behaved in a courageous manner. Not once did a passenger panic or create any problem or distraction for the aircrew. Think about it—what if you were a passenger on that flight, suffering in the extreme cold and oppressive darkness, in fear and uncertainty?

"I did, however, think about the passengers and what it must be like for them. They had nothing to do for over five hours except worry about the danger of our situation. I did, occasionally, inform Coach Pollard that I was optimistic about making it OK and eventually finding a place to land safely. Actually, the entire episode was easier on the pilots—we had a job to do with no time to think of anything other than flying and finding a way to a safe landing."

On the subject of heroes, I introduced my older brother, Earl, who with his wife, was seated in the rear of the room. "Earl, after learning of the death of our older brother, Quentin, at Pearl Harbor, had joined the Navy. Earl became a gunner on a torpedo bomber that was shot down and crashed on the beach on Saipan

Island as the Marines were storming ashore. The pilot had struck the instrument panel and was knocked unconscious. Earl and another crew member pulled the pilot from the burning airplane just before it exploded." A standing applause greeted my brother.

I pointed to my son, Doug, and his wife, Sandy. "Meet another hero from the war in Vietnam. My son, Doug, was serving on a destroyer off the coast of Vietnam when a shell exploded in a gun turret. Without hesitation, he helped pull a sailor from the turret while the danger of another explosion existed.

"One of you had asked what it takes to be a good pilot and this is what I told him. The physical part of flying can be learned by nearly anyone in a short time—getting the airplane started and into the air, around and down again safely. That part of flying we call stick and rudder represents only about five percent of the business of flying. The other ninety-five percent is common sense and judgment. Knowledge of existing and forecast weather is a paramount factor whenever we fly as you can determine from the flight we are commemorating tonight.

"I had been fortunate to have an opportunity to fly for the Army Air Corps and Air Force for many years prior to 1960. During this time, I spent many hours in emergency and safety training in classrooms, flight simulators and in the air. Make no mistake about it, there is no substitute for experience and training." I joked about when a pilot runs out of airspeed, altitude and ideas simultaneously he has a problem. "Fortunately for us, this was avoided by finding a place to land here in Carroll before running out of fuel.

"In my opinion, flying is a very serious business, especially when you are paid to fly passengers. As pilots, we are morally responsible to devote our efforts to doing all that we can to ensure their safety. The landscape has been littered over the years with mangled flying machines and bodies as a result, in general, of poor judgment or lack of experience. Thank God that we are here tonight and not remembered only in the archives of newspapers.

"Jim did a good job of covering the flight but I want to go on record saying, Thank you, Carroll. Without your bright lights, the cornfield would not have been as visible and inviting. Your snow plowing crews had kept highway 71 open enough for us to follow it. Hopefully the Iowa Highway department will consider straightening out the highway north of town where we lost it just in case something like this happens again. Fate had a hand in leading us to Carroll in the heartland of America, where exists a microcosm of the true foundation of America. Few people living in large cities know of your culture of neighborliness, friendliness, and being willingly accommodating.

"Thank you all for inviting us, and now I smell fresh coffee to go with that cake."

John said, "Before the cake, we have to unveil the memorial plaque." Jim and I had the honor of unveiling the memorial plaque which would be mounted in the Veteran's Memorial Park near where we had landed fifty years ago this night. After the unveiling, we enjoyed the cake provided by the Chamber of Commerce ladies. The friendly folks gathered around, asking questions and graciously thanking us for being there. After a brief conversation, it seemed that I had known them for a long time. There were several reporters present from newspapers, television and radio stations who had been taking photos and recording. This was the beginning of a flurry of media activity and changing of my life for the next few years.

While speaking, I had complained of having a stiff neck, saying I had recently seen a chiropractor for a back problem and he had screwed up my neck. Dr. Donovan, a chiropractor, later introduced himself and offered to drive me to his nearby clinic where he skillfully relieved my discomfort with an adjustment free of charge, and then he drove me to the hotel. This was a prime example of the spirit of these good people.

After a restful night, we were gathered in the hotel lobby checking out. Jim approached me, placing his hands on my shoulders and looked me straight in the eyes. "Giff, how about a big hug?" As we embraced, Jim said, "Thank you, old friend, for helping to save my life."

"Helping is correct as it was your alertness that made it happen," I replied.

Jim said, "We're going to be good buddies as long as we live."

"You can count on it, Jim," I said.

Our gang met at a nearby café for breakfast. We then drove to the Veteran's Memorial Park where the commemorative plaque would later be mounted. We had been informed that the exact spot where our airplane finally came to a stop was within fifty yards of where the memorial plaque would be mounted. While standing there, I thought of the great joy and celebrating that had occurred fifty years ago as we all safely crawled out of the airplane into snow up to our knees. My son Doug said, "I bet I know what you are thinking with that far-away look in your eyes."

"Just think about it," I said. "It was this very spot that the crowning event of half a century of flying occurred, plus the miraculous fifty-year extension of my life."

My dear wife Carol added, "Had you not survived we would never have met."

My brother Earl said, "How many would never have been born if you had gone into those trees."

I said, "Let's drive to the town of Auburn and see if we can find that stand of old trees." After taking several pictures of the famous location and the Veteran's Memorial we headed north on highway 71. Only twelve miles north of Carroll—covered in five minutes in the DC-3—is the quaint little town of Auburn with a population of nearly three hundred. As we entered Auburn, we could see, just ahead, the large sign with an arrow pointing west and the number 71 in the center, just as I had imagined it. We parked and took pictures of this memorable location. As I stood shivering on this bleak and foggy day, I saw in the distance the fog-shrouded tops of a large stand of old trees. That had to be the spot where we nearly ended it all.

Why stand in the cold looking at old trees? It's similar to a scene from John Grisham's book, "Bleachers." A group of middle-aged men, mostly former teammates of the state champions, the Spartans of Messina, Texas, gathered in the bleachers of their old high school stadium. They had returned to their hometown fifteen years after that Championship game to bury their coach, the man who had molded them into an unbeatable dynasty. As they sat drinking beer, they awaited the darkening of the stadium, signaling the coach's passing. They listened to a tape of the winning game, reliving the miracle play in which their all-American quarterback, Neely Crenshaw, scored the winning touchdown as time was running out.

The trophy, publicity, fame and a lifetime of memories that they received as a reward paled in comparison to the rewards that we received for our miracle landing. In that game, fifty years ago, in a real life or death struggle, I was proud to have recovered the fumble that lead to a winning "touchdown," as time was running out, not in the end zone but in a cornfield. A summary of our rewards was, for myself, an added fifty years plus of a wonderful life doing what I enjoyed most, flying. For twenty-two others, an award of an extended lifespan, and for those who would never have been born, life itself. It just doesn't get much better than that.

As we headed back to Carroll, I noticed the lack of obstructions in the area in which I did the maneuvering so close to the ground that stormy night. There seemed to be an abundance of level farm fields in the vicinity where we might have been able to land safely had we run out of fuel. After the final farewells before leaving Carroll, we followed the route back home that we had traveled in the bus fifty years ago.

* * * * *

## Radio Shows and Phone Calls

Back home again, unusual events began to occur in my life. Here I was pushing ninety, an age that many folks find themselves occupied with such things as making burial arrangements, or deciding what to have done with their ashes, looking at assisted living communities and updating their last will and testament. The boost to my ego at the reunion had given me a renewed interest in life and the world of adventure.

As the thrill of notoriety began to subside, I received a phone call from a local radio station, asking if I would be available for a live radio broadcast on their hourly sports talk program. Arrangements were made for a date and time that they would call me at home and patch me into their show. Some big name sportscasters were involved and it went off without a problem and was a lot of fun for me. Soon I was receiving calls from various newspapers from around the area for interviews. Due to the publicity, I had begun to hear from people from my past that had helped to renew old acquaintances.

One particular call was of special interest to me as it filled in a part of my story that had been missing until now. The call was from Paul Tobin, a retired air traffic controller. Paul said that his duty station was at Omaha, Nebraska, where he was serving as a RAPCON (Radio Approach Control) operator. Paul said that he had come on duty at midnight on January 18, 1960, and had been informed by Kansas City Center that an unidentified aircraft had just entered his area of surveillance. The aircraft had popped up on their screen and they had no way of positively identifying it. Paul tracked the target until it disappeared from his screen at about twenty miles south of Carroll at around one a.m. That would perfectly coincide with the time that we had descended from four thousand five hundred feet altitude to near the surface where Paul's radar could no longer track us. When he later heard of our landing at Carroll, he knew who his target had been.

Another call came from Verne Smith, a mechanic and aircraft service man for Gopher Aviation. Verne had been dispatched to Carroll with a crew to repair the airplane and arrange for an emergency air strip to facilitate getting the airplane out of there. Verne's big complaint was that damn thirty feet of barbed wire that had wound itself around the tail wheel after snapping when we had hit it. He and his crew did a great job. After replacing the generators and batteries and refueling they arranged for a bull-dozer to remove and pack the snow on a nearby field. They towed the airplane to the downwind end of their runway and soon it was on the way back to home base.

I received a call from Jim Harzog who had lived in Carroll at the time we landed there. Jim was the guy who had heard our noisy airplane and jumped out of bed, putting a snowsuit on over his pajamas and heading out the door. Jim's car got stuck in the snow and he hitched a ride to town on a fire truck and began helping the police to have everyone turn their yard lights on. Later that morning, at the hotel where local folks showed up to congratulate us and wish us well, Jim was there too.

Jim and I later got together in my home and he gave me several laminated photos from the front page of the Carroll newspaper and a copy of the placemat that all on board the airplane had signed. I still have the pictures and I've had several copies made to distribute to friends.

# 16

# VETERAN'S MEMORIAL PARK BASKETBALL COURT DEDICATION

Meanwhile, in Carroll, John Steffes had embarked on another project that created a renewal of media attention. John had contacted Jeanie Buss, Operations manager and Vice President for the Los Angeles Lakers, with a special request. The city of Carroll, moved by John's promotional skills, planned to build a basketball court within the Veteran's Memorial Park near where we had landed in 1960. John offered Jeanie Buss and the Lakers an opportunity to be involved. Jeanie had responded with a very generous offer of twenty-five thousand dollars to help cover the cost. John's brother, a contractor, had donated labor and material as others pitched in to complete the project.

A dedication of the basketball court was scheduled for September 13, 2010, to which I had received an invitation. Others who would attend included Jeanie Buss, Tommy Hawkins (a Minneapolis Laker who had been on the flight in 1960), Steve Springer (sports editor covering the L.A. Lakers for twenty-five years) and many news reporters including a representative of the NBA.

My wife, Carol, and I were driven to Carroll by my stepson, Mark, and our two grandsons, Brett and Drew. We had received a warm welcome and greeting by many Carroll officials, especially John Steffes and Mayor Pedelty.

Norm Hutcheson, the airport commissioner, had made arrangements with a Michigan Yankee Air Force unit to have a C-47 (the Air Force version of the DC-3) on the airport ramp. The fly-in breakfast was a huge success. Jeanie Buss and Tommy Hawkins addressed the crowd as they feasted on pancakes.

I was asked to fly as co-pilot in the Douglas airplane—a highlight of the day. I flew the airplane following Highway 71 north from Carroll to the town of Auburn. As I looked down through the weather window, I could barely see the large sign in the center of Auburn with a large white arrow pointing west for Highway 71—without a doubt this is where I had lost it. A strange feeling came over me as I spotted the trees not far ahead where I had had the scare of my life. As I surveyed the area where I had maneuvered the airplane so close to the ground in the snowstorm, I appreciated that it was so level with no obstructions. During the past fifty years I have relived those moments many times, especially when trying to sleep, watching the clock display 01:40.

The next and greatest highlight of the day was to meet Jeanie Buss and to see Tommy Hawkins again. Carol later said Jeanie was so friendly and gracious, and I agreed. Tommy had some good advice for my grandsons, Brett and Drew, as he told them to practice hard, study hard and they could become great athletes. Tommy was very appreciative to hear, for the first time, accurate details of what had happened that night.

A reporter from the NBA network filmed a news video with myself in the co-pilot seat of the C-47. This was later shown on the NBA channel's inaugural telecast. Steve Springer (author and former editor for the *L.A. Times*) recorded video for a very unique documentary, which is yet to appear on television. Steve and his entire crew later came to my home to do more filming for the documentary.

The main attractions for the dedication of the basketball court were Jeanie Buss and Tommy Hawkins. Their presentations overwhelmed the crowd of happy celebrants as Jeanie Buss cut the ribbon to the court and Tommy Hawkins got on his knees to kiss the hallowed ground on which we were spared, as he said.

Left: Jeanie Buss of the Los Angeles Lakers and myself at the Lakers basketball court dedication ceremony, September, 2010 in Carroll, Iowa.
(Courtesy the *Carroll Daily Times Herald*)

After the ribbon cutting, two sons of John Steffes shot the first baskets on the court. Johnny shot a basket in the north hoop while Robby shot one in the south one. When Tommy Hawkins asked the boys who their favorite team is and Robby said the Celtics, Tommy gave him a hard time.

While having dinner in the hotel café, we were engaged in conversation with a waitress who had vivid memories of that night in

Tommy Hawkins speaking at the Lakers court dedication (above) and then kissing "the hallowed ground upon which we were spared" (below). Seated L to R (below) is John Steffes, myself, and Jeanie Buss. (Courtesy the *Carroll Daily Times Herald*)

January, fearing we would fly into her home. As they had been on our previous visits, the people of Carroll were very friendly and courteous. Someone actually credited us with putting Carroll on the map, but the fact is they put Carroll on the map by lighting up the town and making our landing site more visible.

The next morning was warm and sunny as Mark drove north on Highway 71 to the town of Auburn. As we neared the sign showing the highway turning left, my grandson Brett asked, "Grandpa, did you see this sign when you were up there?" to which Drew, the younger seven-year-old grandson said, "That's a dumb question, Brett, because it was dark and snowing and his windshield was iced up."

"Drew is right, because the snow was blowing all around and it was hard to see anything," I said.

Mark asked, "Where are the trees that you nearly knocked down, Giff?" The visibility was much better than when we had been there in January and I pointed to a long line of trees about two miles ahead. We drove around and were able to get much closer and get some good pictures.

While we stood there in silence gazing at the tall trees, Brett asked, "Were you really scared when you saw the trees out your window, Grandpa?"

Mark chimed in, "If I were you, Giff, I'd be having nightmares from what you went through."

I said, "Yes, Brett, I was really scared; I knew what would have happened if we had hit the trees. It's funny that you mention nightmares, Mark. I was just thinking about a question that Steve Springer asked when he interviewed me for his documentary. He had asked if I'd had nightmares from that scare. My idea of a nightmare was what bomber pilots suffered after WW II. I have a friend who flew a B-24 bomber over Europe and he often saw bombers go down in flames. When no chutes appeared, he knew that his friends were about to die and he would call loudly, 'Get out, get out!' Don still has screaming nightmares of this.

"My answer to Steve's question was no, but I often wake up trying to visualize just what it would have been like to have crashed, and it's not pretty."

Mark had said, "If you had not made it, Giff, I'd never have had you as a stepfather." After high fives all around we loaded up in the SUV and headed north.

Below: Showing my grandsons, Brett and Drew, the line of trees where we almost crashed.

From L to R: Mark Heinlein, Carol Gifford, Tommy Hawkins, Drew Heinlein, Brett Heinlein, Jeanie Buss, and Harold Gifford at the Lakers Court dedication ceremony in Carroll, Iowa, September, 2010. (Courtesy the *Carroll Daily Times Herald*)

# 1 7

# MY SPEAKING TOUR

Within a week of the latest event in Carroll, I received a very welcome phone call from my old friend, Don Rott. Don and I had worked for Gopher Aviation long ago and have been friends for a long while. Don was an airplane salesman and I had managed the flight department. At eighty, he is still selling quality airplanes and is deserving of being known as the world's greatest airplane salesman. I noticed on the caller ID that it was Don and I answered the phone by asking, "Have you sold any airplanes today, Don?" and his answer, as always, was, "No, Giff, but the day isn't over yet. I suppose that after all the notoriety you wouldn't be able to find time to do a favor for an old friend." Don said. "The President of the MBAA (Minnesota Business Aviation Association) Pat Moran and I have talked over the idea and we'd like you to be the guest speaker for our next meeting."

After hearing the time and place for the meeting I jokingly said, "I'm checking over my schedule and yes, I'd be happy to do that."

At the Fort Snelling Officers club, I was surprised to see the large group of pilots and others engaged in the aviation industry gathered for the meeting. Many of those attending were old pilot friends and acquaintances from the many aviation enterprises

145

represented. As a pilot speaking to this group I was in my comfort zone as it was just another hangar flying session.

It had occurred to me that several years prior I had frequently spoken to my squadron and group in this very room. I had been Commander of the 96th squadron of the Active Air Force Reserve and the 934th group and base commander.

Jim Holznagel and his wife were there, as well as Don Rott, his wife, June, and my wife, Carol. Pat Moran was unable to attend because of a scheduled flight. Pat and I had planned to act as though he was a reporter asking questions that I would answer. In his absence Pat had instructed an association officer, Kristi Stengl, to pinchhit for him. She was prepared to ask the questions but after the introduction I hit the power and took off on my own, carelessly ignoring the embarrassed young lady. Afterward I had apologized but Kristi graciously said that she was happy to get out of it.

The feedback from my talk must have been satisfactory, as Pat Moran, president of MBAA, had called and said he wanted to nominate me as a candidate for possible induction to the Minnesota Aviation Hall of Fame. Pat came to my home and gathered information for the process. Pat had developed a slide show presentation and generously gave his time to help in the many presentations that were to come. My friend, Don, and new friend Pat had caused the notoriety activity to kick in again.

Don acted like a booking agent and soon had me set up as the guest speaker for the St. Paul QB (Quiet Birdmen) hangar. Pat, as pilot, had flown non-stop in the Gulfstream Jet from Moscow and made it to the meeting on time with his slide show.

My next speaking gig was for the annual meeting and banquet of the South St. Paul EAA (Experimental Aircraft Association). It was at this meeting that I was privileged to meet Ken Ferguson, who was co-pilot on the Ricky Nelson disaster in 1985 (also in a DC-3). Ken told me some of his story and showed me the scars from the accident and said he'd be speaking at the next meeting of the chapter at Fleming Field. I attended this meeting and was held spellbound as I heard Ken's story.

Pilots, in general, attempt to learn all that they can from the experience of others and follow up on the NTSB (National Transportation Safety Board) investigations and their conclusions as to probable cause of accidents. The NTSB frequently publishes the coroner's report from accidents and reviewing these tend to heighten a pilot's desire to become the best pilot that they can.

Another terrific surprise came in the form of a call from Nancy Novak, secretary for Brian Short. Brian, an attorney, former judge and currently President and CEO of Short Companies—including Admiral Merchants Motor Freight—is a son of the late Bob Short. Nancy had invited me to be the guest speaker for the corporation's annual Eagle awards banquet.

The event was at the Minnesota Twins new baseball stadium in the Metropolitan room. My stepdaughter, Debby, and her husband, Steve, had driven Carol and I as no one in the family would ride with me in downtown Minneapolis after dark. As an added bonus, we were treated to a complete guided tour of the ballpark. My agent, Don, and his wife, June, were on the tour with us. Steve said, "I wouldn't mind working for a company like this. That Brian really knows how to treat his help." We all agreed with that. We had a wonderful dinner and a great time. Speaking to a group of bankers, managers, attorneys and executives is somewhat different from speaking to a group of pilots. I had learned long ago, in a speech class, to choose a topic that you know and love. Meeting those requirements put me in my comfort zone and I was pleased to observe a very attentive group that was enjoying my story.

I found it obvious that Brian had followed in his father's footsteps by surrounding himself with a great and loyal team. Brian genuinely makes people realize that he is enjoying their company; this may be why he is so well liked.

The story in the *Woodbury Magazine* (reprinted in Chapter 18) attracted more attention and soon I received another invitation to tell my story. The chairman of the board of the Woodbury Chamber of Commerce called and invited me to be the guest speaker at the next Chamber luncheon meeting. The chairman offered to pick me up and I thanked him and said that wouldn't be necessary. I'm blessed to have all my original parts with no aftermarket accessories, with the exception of hearing aids, and no walker or wheelchair. The chairman had sought the opinion of a previous host on my speaking tour as to my ability to keep it together long enough for a thirty-minute telling of my story. The response was, "The only problem you may have is shutting him down." As it turned out, that was exactly what he had to do as the Chamber members had to get back to work. That about wrapped up my speaking tour and since a large number of attentive listeners appeared to enjoy hearing my story I decided to share it with others through this book.

# 18

# HANGAR FLYING

Old pilots look forward to and frequently engage in "hangar flying." I guess the term comes from the old days when weather kept pilots on the ground so they just sat around the hangar and talked about flying experiences. Jim and I, for example, have thousands of hours of flying time over a period of fifty years. A few days ago, Jim and I did a bit of hangar flying and the first thing to be discussed was our cornfield landing, trying to reconstruct the events of that day and night. Jim asked, "Giff, why do you think Verne wouldn't go along with our idea to land in the cornfield when it seemed to be a safe bet and our fuel state was critical?"

"Ya know, Jim, I've puzzled over that question for a long time. Maybe having been an aircraft carrier pilot he would never have ditched in the ocean as long as he had some fuel remaining to try to find the carrier. It's a known fact that when under extreme stress, pilots have been known to revert to earlier training and indoctrination."

After sipping on his cup of coffee, Jim, with a quizzical look, shook his head and said, "Another thing, Giff—over the years, I have flown with pilots who had something physically wrong that had definitely caused erratic behavior. One guy in particular had been making questionable decisions and a few years later he died from a brain tumor."

"You just never know, Jim. We have both flown with guys hung over and those with marital or other problems and we know what that's about. I remember a very powerful statement that you had made at one time when we were discussing Verne's early death. I think you said, 'Poor Verne died five minutes after the lights went out that night,' and he actually died five years after that," I remarked. "If Verne had been born in 1921 he had lived only about forty-five years, so I figure we can't begrudge him having basked in the glory for saving all our lives. Why do you think Verne left it up to you and I to find a way out of that mess we were in?"

"It had to be simply that he had no knowledge of the en route weather as he had only checked the destination weather and he knew that you and I had been on top of it all day. He had lacked the important information needed to form a plan of action," Jim said.

\* \* \* \* \*

### Hangar Flying at Its Very Best

As busy as Brian Short is managing his many business enterprises, he is able to find time for an occasional hangar flying lunch at the Lexington on Grand Avenue. At times Brian calls and says, "Giff, I've rounded up some more victims to hear you and Don tell your stories."

Don Rott and I flew for Gopher Aviation in the early sixties. We had often flown together and we both flew the Hughes helicopters. The two of us have a bottomless supply of tales to reminisce over. Don and I have a lot in common as we both came close to dying in an airplane. Don was a passenger in a very bad crash and had to spend many months in hospital being put back together. Don and I frequently have breakfast together at a favorite spot when we relive the "golden years" of private aviation.

I believe that research would prove my friend to be the world's greatest aircraft salesman. Don has sold over 400 Beech Barons, in addition to many other models—and he's still making deals at 81. Don's success has been due to his reputation for providing purchasers with quality airplanes. Don belongs in the Minnesota Aviation Hall Of Fame and hopefully will soon be there.

The time has come to close the hangar doors, as my wife Carol often reminds us if we put the wives to sleep with our tales. My final advice for pilots: keep the shiny side up and the rubber side down.

* * * * *

## Other Articles and Accounts of the Cornfield Landing

The following are reports of Lakers' stories about the famous flight from their perspective. The repetition of the story serves to show the various opinions on just what happened. Some minor misunderstandings: Verne did not lose his license, we never wore goggles, there was no regulation about landing with the gear retracted, there was no argument about landing gear up or down, there was no ditch ahead of where we landed, there was no frostbite, the passengers were not told that we were lost and about to run out of fuel, we had not attempted to land on a road when it was said that a truck was in the way, and we did not come close to power lines. There was only one landing attempt and it was the successful one. There are many other inaccurate reports and assumptions. It is understandable how uncertainty and imagination can play a part in these unfounded assumptions.

## The Flight As Reported by Bob Leonard
(Re-printed with permission of Steve Aschburner, NBA.com)

Somehow, the headline on the website of the Carroll, Iowa *Daily Times Herald*—"Carroll to celebrate 50th anniversary of Minneapolis Lakers' forced airplane landing here"—seems a little off. Celebrate? A forced landing? It seems more like something you'd rather wipe from your memory altogether: possibly the closest call in NBA history and one of the league's most harrowing incidents.

Then again, it was a big deal in Carroll, a town of about 10,000 folks in western Iowa along the Middle Raccoon River. That night 50 years ago—January 18, 1960—put Carroll on the map, you might say, because of how close the Lakers came to being put—*splat!*—literally on the map themselves.

Besides, when you get past the frightful sequence of events on the team's old DC-3 aircraft, you remember that, in aviation, a forced landing from which everyone walks away beats the alternative 100 times out of 100. The Lakers, the pilots and the civilians on board kept on going, living their lives, many of them for all of the half-century since.

Take Bobby "Slick" Leonard, for instance. Leonard was 27 at

the time, in his fourth season with the Lakers, a two-time all-American at Indiana and captain of the Hoosiers' 1953 NCAA championship team. He wrapped up his playing career in Chicago in 1962-63 and by 1968-69 had taken over as head coach of the Indiana Pacers, winning three ABA championships and 529 games over 12 seasons as the franchise transitioned into the NBA in 1976-77. He is now in his 25th year as a Pacers broadcaster. One summer in the late 1970s, Leonard hosted a telethon to keep the franchise in Indianapolis. He and his wife Nancy have five children (two born after the unnerving flight) and seven grandchildren.

Much of the above paragraph doesn't happen if pilot Verne Ullman and co-pilot Harold Gifford didn't find that cornfield just outside of Carroll on Hilbert Steffes' farm and set that crippled plane down just so. And that's just one fella's story.

There was another guy on the flight named Elgin Baylor. And a bunch more—Jim Pollard, Frank Selvy, Hot Rod Hundley, Jim Krebs, Tom Hawkins—23 people in all. The Lakers—the organization that would move to Los Angeles a few months later and eventually win nine more NBA titles.

So celebrate? Heck, yes.

"It was a hairy ordeal," Leonard said the other night in Minneapolis. He was back in town to work a Pacers-Timberwolves game and, of course, he could laugh a little now, safe and long-removed from the big scare. At the time, though ...

"From takeoff to the time we hit in that cornfield, we were up there somewhere between two and three hours," Leonard recalled. "We were running out of gas, so they did everything they could to find someplace. It was a snowstorm but when the moon came out, that's when we started buzzing that town. You saw the lights start coming on below us. I heard one of the pilots say, 'That looks like a cornfield. We're gonna have to put it down. We're gonna have to put it down.'"

The Lakers had lost a Sunday afternoon game in St. Louis, 135-119, and were at Lambert Field by about 5:30 p.m., their converted World War II cargo plane ready to go (built in the 1930s, it had been retired by Western Airlines before being purchased by Lakers owner Bob Short). An ice storm grounded all flights, however, for several hours. Eventually the weather broke, the team boarded and the plane took off.

Within minutes, the lights went out. "I thought it was one of our guys joking around," said Pollard, the four-time Lakers All-Star who had taken over as coach two weeks earlier. In Minnesota, author Stew Thornley's book, *Basketball's Original Dynasty: The History of the Lakers*, Pollard (who died in 1993) continued: "But when I got to the front, I saw the co-pilot shining a flashlight on the instrument panel." The twin-engine plane's generators had failed and the battery was drained from waiting out the storm so long on the ground.

"We were flying in the dark, and it was cold as hell," guard Dick Garmaker told the *St. Paul Pioneer Press* in October. From his seat in the front row, Garmaker could see Ullman and Gifford poking their heads out the sliding windows on the sides of the cockpit due to the frosted windshield. The pilots took the DC-3 high in an attempt to get over the storm but the unpressurized cabin limited that option. So they took the plane down low to within 200 feet of the ground.

Ullman and Gifford spotted lights, then a water tower. They made several passes, "buzzing" the town in hopes of finding an airstrip or waking the residents for help of some sort. With the gauges dead, the plane's remaining fuel became an issue. The pilots decided to risk a landing and scouted for a suitable road. At one point, Ullman had to pull up to avoid a cluster of trees. Then they saw a cornfield north of the town and, having grown up on farms, they knew it would be relatively level. Bad weather that fall had kept the owner from harvesting, so the corn stalks stood tall.

Here's where a story about Baylor, perhaps apocryphal, kicks in. Then in his second season, the eventual Hall of Famer reputedly lay down in the aisle near the back of the plane. Some claim Baylor calculated that, if the plane went in nose down, he might simply slide feet-first down the aisle. Others recall him saying something like, "If we're going to crash, I might as well go comfortably."

Leonard can't confirm or deny the tale. "Because it was so cold in the plane, me and Hot Rod were sitting there and we had G.I. blankets on our heads, leaning over. We started making passes over Carroll. Then we had to clear high-tension wires, they couldn't read the terrain—there were a lot of things going on. So I didn't have time to turn around and see where Elgin was. But it sounds good and, knowing him, that's Elgin."

Turns out, they all went comfortably. The snow, the corn stalks, Ullman's skill and the fact that the tail wheel hooked on a strand of the farm's barbed-wire fence all combined for a safe, cushioned landing. "We jumped off. The snow was up to our chests in that cornfield," Leonard said. "I rode into town in the back of a hearse. They had all the red lights flashing, the emergency vehicles, all the police they had."

Leonard also noticed something dead ahead in the plane's path that, in his many re-tellings, gets a little closer and a little deeper each time. "The next day, we took a bus to Minneapolis. We went out there and saw it; if we had gone, I'd say, another 40 or 50 yards, we'd have gone off into a ravine."

Short dispatched mechanics to repair the plane, then hired a bulldozer to clear a runway, enabling Ullman to fly the DC-3 out a few days later. "Then in April," Leonard said, setting up a rest-of-the-story kicker worthy of Paul Harvey, "we're in the playoffs. We go out here to the airport and there's that damn plane sitting there. Same plane! The guys said, 'We're not getting on that.' And Short said, 'You don't get on, you don't have a job.' So we got on. Well, we figured lightning wouldn't strike twice."

That's where most versions of this nerve-wracking episode end. I prefer the scene at the retirement hotel in Carroll where the Lakers were deposited for the night.

"Here's all these old ladies and old men—at that time, we were young—in their nightgowns," Leonard said. "They wanted to see what was going on. They had a little bar with about eight chairs around it, and there was a liquor cabinet. They had a padlock on that liquor cabinet, and old Larry Foust (a 6-foot-9 center from LaSalle)——Larry's passed away now—he went over there and twisted that sonuvabitch right off of there. He got himself a fifth of VO (Canadian whiskey) and poured himself a big glass."

With all due respect to Carroll and its anniversary Monday, *that* is how you celebrate a forced landing.

### *Busy Making His Own Luck*—Dick Garmaker's Story

By Jimmie Tramel, *World* sports writer

(Re-printed with permission of *Tulsa World*)

A team plane carrying the NBA's Minneapolis Lakers slammed into a snow-covered Iowa cornfield nearly 50 years ago. The first person who greeted glad-to-be-alive passengers after they exited the plane was a mortician.

"He was ready to do business," Richard Garmaker said. "He thought he had a lot of business."

The mortician got shut-out that night by the Lakers, who suffered zero casualties.

Garmaker, a Minnesota native who has lived in Tulsa the last 19 years, was among the players who walked away from the emergency landing and, if you ask him, he will tell you he is extremely lucky—at cards and love and maybe even real estate and life.

Garmaker, 76, is a four-time NBA All-Star who played six seasons with the Lakers and Knicks in the 1950s and 1960s. He cut his career short because he discovered he could make a better living in real estate. When he first began dabbling in real estate, he said he made $25,000 with one swipe of an ink pen. That's $3,000 more than he made his final year with the Knicks.

Lucky at cards? Garmaker was allegedly such a card shark that a clause in his last Knicks contract prohibited him from picking up a deck. Management didn't want to risk the possibility of chemistry being spoiled by Garmaker emptying teammates' pockets at card tables.

Lucky at love? Garmaker picked his wife out of a newspaper when he was 16. He saw a photo of beauty queens riding a parade float in a Minnesota town not far from his own. He knew someone from the town and asked if he could be introduced to the damsel in the photo. He met Darlene in a sweet shop and told her he was going to marry her in eight years. He married her in seven.

Lucky at life? Garmaker said he has done some things in the business world that probably required an element of luck in order to work. Enough things went right in business dealings that he was able to move to a beachfront condo in Naples, Florida; then he pulled up stakes and followed sons Steven and Stuart to Tulsa after they got jobs here.

But the luckiest Garmaker ever got was being given an extra half-century—and still counting—to live.

The Lakers easily could have perished in that DC-3, a converted World War II plane that transported the team to road games. A pilot once told Garmaker the DC-3 was the safest plane in the world because he could land it in a cornfield if necessary. Vernon Ullman and his co-pilot ultimately got the chance to prove it.

The plane departed St. Louis in a winter storm and, shortly after takeoff, lost electrical power. Passengers sat in the dark and covered themselves in blankets as the cabin temperature fell.

The pilot, minus instrumentation or radio assistance, flew north in hopes the storm would clear and they could spot a place to land, according to Garmaker. The storm was still going strong when fuel ran low, so the decision was made to dip below clouds and look for a possible landing area.

Visibility was poor because of snow. The pilot and co-pilot took turns sticking their faces out a cockpit window so they could see, according to Garmaker. Attempted landings were aborted twice and the pilot hit the throttle to rise above danger—first an oncoming semi truck and then high wires.

The plane had been circling Carroll, Iowa, and by the time it landed, ambulances—and an undertaker—were waiting.

Jim Krebs, who sat next to Garmaker on the plane, authored a first-person account of the emergency landing for a June 23, 1969 issue of Sports Illustrated. Wrote Krebs, "Garmaker and I ran off through the knee-deep snow toward a group of cars that had appeared on a road about half a mile away. The first vehicle we reached at the front of the line was a hearse. I'm positive I detected a slightly disappointed look when the driver found out everyone was all right."

Garmaker said the scary plane ride changed him "quite a bit." He said he became more aware of his mortality and got a pilot's license so he could land a plane if necessary. He never had to get on the DC-3 again because he was traded to the Knicks ten days after the plane hit the cornfield. He said he has no fear of flying and has taken many "puddle jumper" planes on hunting and fishing trips.

"The biggest lesson is don't take everything for granted," he said. "Things can happen so quickly and you never know what day is going to be your last."

Both of Garmaker's sons (and a grandson) were born after the crash. He said he has enjoyed life "tremendously" since. Many of his favorite days were spent with sons on outdoor expeditions. They just got back from a trip to Minnesota.

All crash survivors haven't been as fortunate. Garmaker mentioned the names of ex-teammates who have died or are in poor health. Krebs, who always told teammates he was going to die by age 33, died at 30 when he was cutting down a neighbor's tree and the tree fell on him. Krebs also told teammates they shouldn't board that plane in 1960 because something bad was going to happen.

The 50-year anniversary of the crash will be next January 17th.

"If someone decides it would be nice to get together, I would like that," Garmaker said. "If there is a reunion, I would love to go and see who remembers exactly."

## Recollections from those involved

### Brian Short

My dad owned the Minneapolis Lakers, and I remember all the commotion on the night of January 17, 1960. I was nearly ten years old at the time, and what I remember most of all is my dad's concern that his Lakers may have been wiped out in a plane crash. Not only was the team on that airplane, but my dad's business partner, Frank Ryan and his family. We were very much relieved upon learning of their being alive and unharmed.

I now realize how fortunate it was that there were some farm boys in that cockpit. They could see the cornrows and they knew from experience that there would be no obstructions such as rocks or ditches. Really, those pilots, just to get to Carroll, Iowa, took an immense amount of skill that I'm not certain exists in cockpits today. Their being able to translate that into putting the airplane on the ground safely without hurting anyone or damaging the airplane really is a miracle landing.

That's obviously something that wouldn't happen today. Could you imagine a commercial airliner doing that and then flying it out of there? It's inconceivable, but that's what they did and that's the kind of thing those pilots did in those days.

Professional sports teams were folding rampantly in those days. If the flight hadn't turned out as it did, the Minneapolis Lakers would have undoubtedly folded and gone out of existence. There wouldn't have been all the litigation as in this era. One of the team owners would have been wiped out, as well as the coach and team. It would have wiped out the schedule for the rest of the season. The chance of that team coming back would have been close to zero.

**Tommy Hawkins**

After having lost to the Hawks with Bob Petit, Cliff Hagen and their gang, we had dinner at the airport Café. We got on the plane just before eight p.m. and left St. Louis, flying into a snowstorm. Soon after becoming airborne we were bouncing around in turbulence when the lights dimmed, flickered, went bright and then out. It became totally dark in the cabin, and suddenly a flashlight was turned on by the co-pilot. We learned that we had lost both generators and the ship's batteries were dead. We had no lights, no heat or de-icing, none of that. The pilots decided to follow the North Star and try to get over the storm to better weather but after awhile they could climb no higher because we had no oxygen system. The pilots had to avoid icing by staying out of the clouds. They eventually flew low enough where there was snow but too cold for ice forming on the airplane.

I was sitting in the back of the airplane with Bobby Leonard, the All-American from Indiana, and we were talking about making it or not making it. Bob said, "Sure we're going to make it." It was a harrowing time as we were in total darkness, except when on top of the clouds the moon gave us enough light to see and recognize one another. We weren't just in a storm, we were in a blizzard—a Midwest blizzard. Ice had formed on the windows and the floor of the airplane, it was freezing cold—we didn't know where we were and it was horrible.

Just think about the role Carroll, Iowa played in the history of the Lakers, which had become one of the greatest sports franchises in world history. Had we not landed safely the entire history of the NBA would have been changed.

By turning on their lights, the people of Carroll made the cornfield more visible and they responded immediately, fearing that we needed help. They helped us in every way possible after we had landed and even provided us with a great breakfast in the morning."


## Jack Donavan

I was awakened by this loud roar and it sounded as though it would fly right into our house. It seemed to be circling the water tower and I thought they were looking for an airport as they circled in wider arcs. They were gone for a period of ten minutes or so and then returned. The airplane had either crashed or landed on the edge of town and my neighbor Verne Jergens had pulled up along the road near where it had gone down. Verne could hear the hollering and screaming assuming there was chaos and dying passengers. All of a sudden he saw these people wading through the deep snow coming toward him and they were all OK. He then saw the airplane sitting in the cornfield. It was like a miracle and those pilots should have the same recognition as those landing in the Hudson River.

## Helen Quinn, Carroll telephone operator

We had heard the airplane circling the water tower and it was noticed they had no lights on the airplane. We knew for sure that they were in trouble but there wasn't much that we could do. People were alerted to turn on all the lights that they could in hopes that would help. It turned out that the lights had helped the pilots to better see the field and aided the responders to see them after the landing. After they all had arrived at the Burke Motor Hotel we were relieved to know they were all safe as they began calling home. The ladies auxiliary of the Elks Club made breakfast for them. Those pilots really deserve a lot of credit for preventing what could have been a tragedy.

## Doug Gifford, Director, N. Florida Safety Council

I was twelve years old when my mother answered a persistently ringing telephone around midnight on January 17, 1960. I woke up and heard my mother crying and asked her what was going on, and through nearly hysterical sobs she told me that Dad's airplane was missing. That's about all that she knew. My sister Gaylyn and brother John were awake by now and when they heard what was going on our house was a scene of bedlam. Just imagine, the four of us being awakened around midnight with such a disturbing situation.

Dad had been flying since before I was born and I knew that he had a reputation for being an excellent pilot with a good record. We knew that he had to fly in all kinds of weather but we sort of got used to him coming home so we didn't worry very much. The three of us kids were in a Catholic school but Mom was not much into religion so we tried to calm her by praying for Dad's safety.

My dad had been more than just a dad. We were fishing buddies and had hunted pheasants together. Dad had bought a bowling alley so that he could spend more time flying with the Air Force Reserve. I had the opportunity to set pins and earn money and I bowled on a kid's team. Dad had a small airplane and I got to fly with him and even fly the airplane a little. Dad went to my Little League games when he could and helped me practice to improve my playing skills. At one time Dad was a propane distributor and I loved going with him in his big truck and helping him. What I enjoyed most was lunchtime when we'd go to a café and I could order off the menu. If Dad wasn't coming home it would have been unbearable.

Around two a.m. the phone rang again and we all expected to hear the bad news. Mom answered and I can still remember her saying, 'I was afraid that you had crashed and you wouldn't be coming home.' Just imagine the range of emotions over a two-hour period.

When my dad was on the news I was really popular in school with all my friends. Having been a Star/Tribune paperboy, I remember being impressed by the huge front page aerial photo of the plane sitting in the snow-filled Iowa cornfield. My friends were astonished! I was very proud of my dad and always have been for his accomplishments throughout his lifetime.

**Douglas Burns, in the Carroll Daily Times Herald**

The next time you see L.A. Lakers guard Kobe Bryant soaring for a dunk on TV, you may want to take a rooting interest. And yes, that goes for you, too, Celtics fans.

**Vince Irlbeck, Carroll resident, on seeing the Laker DC-3 the next day**

It was unbelievable. What the hell is that plane doing in the middle of a cornfield?

**Roman Steffes, Carroll resident, on hearing the Laker DC-3 in the middle of the night**

It was snowing like the dickens. We were in bed. I said to my wife, 'There's trouble out there for that plane.' We were thinking, just a few months earlier (in September 1959), Soviet leader Khrushchev was in Carroll county at a farm in Coon Rapids—were the Russians back?

**Dick Garmaker, 1960 Laker**

There will always be a soft spot in my heart for the community of Carroll, Iowa. We did not have just two minutes to consider our fate, as the people did on the Hudson River flight, but four long hours before we began to awaken the residents from their slumber in Carroll. Lights began twinkling as we were ready for that final approach into the cornfield. The memory is still vivid and to this day seems miraculous.

**Norman Schultz, Carroll resident who lived next to the water tower**

It was just a roar. It was obviously very, very low. My first impulse was that they were going to fly right into the house. They kept going around in wider circles. I was just glad they didn't crash into my house.


**Jim Krebs, 1960 Laker**

[Ed. note: Jim Krebs was killed in a freak accident in 1965 after retiring from professional basketball the year before. The following is from the recollection of the author and subsequent accounts of the landing given by Jim Krebs].

Jim Krebs had the reputation for being superstitious as he frequently consulted his Ouija board for guidance and predicting the outcome of situations. It had been known that he had predicted our flight would be bad news. Jim was very intelligent and well educated as demonstrated by his passenger's perspective of the situation during the infamous flight.

Jim was skilled in uniquely describing his fears and discomfort during the five hours and forty minutes flight. Not long after becoming airborne, we were above the clouds with a bright full moon shining on the clouds beneath us. "It looked like hundreds of miles of cotton candy as far as I could see,"[2] Jim recalled. It was so terribly cold in the cabin that he had feared freezing to death. When we had flown at a very high altitude without oxygen, Jim was concerned as

2      "The Night Their Luck Turned", Jim Krebs, *Sports Illustrated*, June 23, 1969.

were others, about difficulty in breathing. To Jim, the nearly total darkness was surreal with the only light being the occasional lighting of a cigarette and the yellowish faint glow of a flashlight in the cockpit being used to view the instrument panel. All were huddled under blankets and coats and the children were sleeping most of the time. Jim had attempted to suppress his fears by mentally reciting prayers hoping for providential intercession. The thought of his wife and baby daughter losing him was extremely frightening. When we were flying above the clouds with a full moon above, his spirits were en-kindled as passengers could then see and recognize one another.

Upon learning that we were about to descend, in an attempt to have visual contact with the ground and try to find somewhere to safely land, Jim admitted that he knew the danger involved but understood that to be the best option. When we finally established visual contact with the ground, Jim had become hopeful that we could possibly find a place to land safely though all he could see out his window was fence rows, farm houses, barns silos and windmills. When we finally found a town and began circling it, Jim said it looked like Times Square with people looking up at us in wonder. Jim remembered hearing the co-pilot exclaim, "There is a cornfield on the very edge of town and I think we should land there now before we run out of gas." When the other passengers heard of this, they all became excited as they believed that the aircrew could and would land in the cornfield. Then suddenly a sense of doom and gloom came over the cabin as an ominous cloud when they were again enveloped in darkness and headed into an unknown void of blowing snow and near total darkness. Suddenly there was an abrupt pull-up as the engines roared with increased power as our attempt to land on a road was thwarted by a semi truck having been in the way, Jim recalled. With the ground no longer in sight, it was back to serious prayer and soon it seemed we were being heard as the ground was again in view. In a few minutes we were back over the town and Jim could see the cornfield as the pilots discussed landing there. "We were advised to prepare for what could be a rough landing and soon we heard the corn ears banging the airplane belly as we made a soft landing in the deep snow and corn stalks," Jim recalled. "This had to be the night that our luck changed, as the team soon moved to Los Angeles and after a time, began a new sports dynasty,"[3] Jim later thought.

Sadly, Jim had died in a tragic accident a few years later while he was helping his neighbor remove a fallen tree from his yard.

\* \* \* \* \*

A pleasant surprise was an interview by Debbie Musser, an extremely talented editor for the *Woodbury Magazine*. Her story appeared in her magazine last March (2012) and she really treated me kindly, another big shot to the ego. I'm no spring chicken, not far from ninety, but I'm loving it. Who wouldn't?

---

3      Ibid.

### *Field of Miracles: Carroll Cornfield Airplane Landing*

Former pilot Harold Gifford recalls a famous, harrowing landing in an Iowa cornfield.

By Debbie Musser, March 2012, *Woodbury Magazine*. (reprinted with permission)

Imagine flying an airplane in a rough Midwest snowstorm with no heat, no defroster, no lights, no radio, no fuel gauge and no navigation system.

Harold "Giff" Gifford, a Woodbury resident with a stellar flying career, was co-pilot on a famous 5 hour, 40 minute flight that experienced those daunting challenges. "Though it all occurred over 52 years ago, the events are etched in my memory vividly," says Gifford, 88.

On a Sunday evening—January 17, 1960—a 1935 DC-3 carrying the Minneapolis Lakers basketball team left St. Louis' Lambert Field en route to Minneapolis. "Shortly after takeoff, both generators failed while we were in the clouds, and we soon realized that we were in a lot of trouble," says Gifford. "Weather briefings led me to believe that by getting to Des Moines, we'd find good weather ahead."

Following the North Star, the pilots kept climbing to get above the ice-laden clouds. Above 15,000 feet altitude, they had to reverse course out of the cloud tops, then turn west to go around the storm. This plan also failed. "The only choice remaining involved a bold and daring plan to enter the clouds and descend below the icing level with our limited altimeter and rate of climb/descent indicator instruments," says Gifford. "If we were lucky, we'd find better weather before fuel starvation."

## The Passengers

Nine Lakers players, who had lost to the St. Louis Hawks earlier that day, were aboard the harrowing flight: Elgin Baylor, Boo Ellis, Larry Foust, Dick Garmaker, Tommy Hawkins, Rod Hundley, Jim Krebs, Bob Leonard and Frank Selvy. Also aboard were Coach Jim Pollard and his 11-year-old son as well as nine men, women and children associated with team ownership and management. All were soon huddled together in the dark, cold cabin as ice began to form on the windows and floor of the plane.

"Amazingly, no one seemed to panic," says Garmaker, a 1955 All-American for the University of Minnesota Golden Gophers who was an NBA All-Star with the Lakers, and also played for the New York Knicks. "Somehow we all felt that we were going to make it."

## A Saving Light

Gifford and captain Verne Ullman (now deceased) were at the controls of the DC-3, making decisions as time was running out. Luckily, there was someone else in the cockpit: 21-year-old Jim Holznagel, who has just started a job flying for Gopher Aviation. "I was in the jump seat between the captain and the co-pilot to observe as I had not flown a DC-3 before," he says.

Holznagel served a critical role as the pilots steered through the stormy night in total darkness, shining flashlights and penlights on the instrument panel hour after hour as the fuel state became crucial. They decided to risk a descent to (hopefully) find a suitable landing spot. "The pilots took turns putting their heads out their side cockpit windows looking for the ground," says Holznagel.

"Jim held the light on the altimeter and rate of descent, calling out numbers," says Gifford. Around 1 a.m., over five hours after departure and nearing 500 feet altitude, Gifford eventually caught site of farm lights, then a blacktop road leading to a town. As they repeatedly circled the town, lights kept coming on: people knew they were in trouble. "The lights helped illuminate an unpicked cornfield nearby—a possible landing site," says Gifford. "However, there was a difference of opinion so we headed north in search of an airport or better weather, though we had to have been very low on fuel."

Then, while flying, Gifford lost the road, saying "I lost it" to Ullman, who said "I have it!" "Verne had the controls, not the road, and soon I saw we were losing altitude and nearly in a grove of trees," says Holznagel, who called that out as Gifford grabbed the controls, barely missing the trees, then climbing into the clouds, turning and locating the road, which led back to the town.

That town was Carroll, Iowa, surrounded by farmland. "We decided that cornfield would be the best place to land as the corn was unpicked, which gave us some depth perception," says Holznagel.

With only about 15 minutes of fuel left, the plane landed safely in that snow-covered cornfield. "All at once I heard the sound of the corn stalks hitting the bottom of the airplane," says Holznagel. "We came to a stop in a very short time as the deep snow slowed the plane down."

"I remember that it was a really smooth landing, and we opened the doors to very deep snow and a road lined with cars, ambulances and hearses," says Garmaker. "As I reflect on that landing, I think about how lucky we were to have the competent pilots that we had, especially Harold. I was sitting up close to the cockpit and had a firsthand view of what was going on."

## A Full Life

Later that same year, the Lakers moved to Los Angeles to become the NBA's first West Coast team. Gifford continued flying, then moved on to stock and real estate sales in Florida where he also operated Giff's Sub Shops in Fort Walton Beach and Destin before returning to Minnesota, where he resumed flying charter and corporate airplanes. He retired from flying in 1993, the same year he and his wife Carol moved to Woodbury.

"My life has been one big adventure," says Gifford. "When I think about that day in 1960, I believe that fate had something to do with it. Had we not made it, there may not have been an L.A. Lakers franchise. More importantly, there wouldn't be 23 families with kids and grandkids living today.

"I've also thought about what it would have been like to hit those trees. It would have been like getting hit in the face with a baseball bat."

Gifford is writing a book about the Carroll landing experience, The Miracle Landing. "I've retold the story so many times, and I will include other experiences from my Air Force and charter flying days," he says. "I'm proud that, through my training, I was given an opportunity to help save lives that night, and I was able to keep cool and got 'er done."

Today Gifford truly enjoys a full life (he lists many hobbies, including a favorite: cooking). But most of all, he enjoys his coffee each day with Carol, his wife of 40 years. "We reflect on how lucky we are; we're very joyful," says Gifford. "As I like to say, life is so darn good. I couldn't live without it."

---

*Lives of great men all remind us*

*We can make our lives sublime*

*And in passing leave behind us*

*Footprints on the sands of time*

—"A Psalm of Life"
H.W. Longfellow

CPSIA information can be obtained at www.ICGtesting.com
Printed in the USA
BVOW100100050613

322233BV00004B/20/P